FROM THE COSMOS TO THE CROSS

A TEEN'S GUIDE TO EXPLORING THE EVIDENCE FOR GOD AND JESUS

CYRIL OPOKU

FROM THE COSMOS TO THE CROSS

From the Cosmos to the Cross: A Teen's Guide to Exploring the Evidence for God and Jesus

© 2025 Cyril Opoku. TeenCompass Collective. All rights reserved.

No part of this book may be reproduced, stored in a retrieval system, or transmitted in any form or by any means—electronic, mechanical, photocopying, recording, or otherwise—without the prior written permission of the publisher, except for brief quotations used in reviews, articles, or other non-commercial purposes as permitted by copyright law.

All Scripture quotations, unless otherwise indicated, are taken from:

Scripture quotations marked (NIV) are taken from the Holy Bible, New International Version®, NIV®. Copyright ©1973, 1978, 1984, 2011 by Biblica, Inc.™ Used by permission. All rights reserved worldwide.

Scripture quotations marked (ESV) are taken from the ESV® Bible (The Holy Bible, English Standard Version®), copyright © 2001 by Crossway, a publishing ministry of Good News Publishers. Used by permission. All rights reserved.

Scripture quotations marked (NKJV) are taken from the New King James Version®.

Copyright © 1982 by Thomas Nelson. Used by permission. All rights reserved.

Published by *Quest Publications (questpublications@outlook.com)*

Cover design & Interior layout by *Quest Publications*

ISBN: 978-1-988439-55-6

Printed in the United States of America

First Edition: June 2025

For more books like this, visit *TeenCompass Collective:* https://teencompasscollective.org

Contents

PART ONE: THE COSMOS

Chapter 1. Did the Big Bang Prove God Exists? 3

Chapter 2. Who Made God? (And Does It Even Matter?) 11

Chapter 3. Did the Universe Have a Beginning? 18

Chapter 4. So Saturn Is How Old? Is Infinity Just a Big Lie? 25

Chapter 5. Is the Universe a Giant Coincidence... Or Did Someone Design It for Us? 32

Chapter 6. If Math is a Language, Who's Speaking? 39

Chapter 7. Why Is There Something Rather Than Nothing? 46

Chapter 8. Can You Be Good Without God? 53

Chapter 9. Could God Be Like...A Pizza? 60

Chapter 10. Can Evil and Suffering Really Cancel Out God? 67

Chapter 11. Can You Actually Know God? Like, Really Know Him? 74

PART TWO: THE CROSS

Chapter 12. Did Jesus Really Exist? 84

Chapter 13. What Did Jesus Actually Look Like? And Does It Even Matter? 95

Chapter 14. Did Jesus Claim To Be God? 102

Chapter 15. Did Jesus Really Die on the Cross? 109

Chapter 16. Did Jesus Really Rise from the Dead? The Evidence You Can't Ignore! 119

Chapter 17. Why Was Jesus Crucified? It's More Than You Think! 130

Preface

From the Cosmos to the Cross: A Teen's Guide to Exploring the Evidence for God and Jesus

Have you ever sat in class, scrolled through social media, or lay awake at night wondering, *Is this all just random? Does God actually exist? And even if He does... does any of this Jesus stuff really matter to me?*

You're not alone.

In a world where doubt is easy and belief is often mocked, it can feel risky—even weird—to ask big questions about life, truth, and faith. Maybe you've heard things like: "Science has disproved God," or "Jesus is just a myth," or "Believing in God is like believing in unicorns." Maybe you've grown up in church but secretly wonder if any of it's actually real. Or maybe you've walked through pain or loss and thought, *If God is out there, He sure isn't doing a great job.*

This book was written for you.

Not to shut down your questions—but to honor them. Because honest questions deserve honest answers. And you shouldn't have to choose between having a brain and having a faith. God can handle your doubts. In fact, they might just be the doorway to deeper belief.

From the Cosmos to the Cross is a two-part journey.

Part One: The Cosmos explores the evidence for God through the universe, science, morality, math, beauty, and logic. We'll tackle questions like: *Did the Big Bang prove God? Could everything have come from nothing? Why does evil exist if God is good?* And yes… *Could God be like a pizza?*

Part Two: The Cross shifts the focus to the person of Jesus. We'll look at history, archaeology, and biblical records to ask: *Did Jesus really live? Did He claim to be God? Did He actually rise from the dead—and if so, what does that mean for you?*

You don't have to have all the answers to start asking the right questions. You just need curiosity and a willingness to wrestle. This isn't a book filled with complicated theology or fluffy clichés. It's an honest, teen-friendly look at the biggest questions of life, written for real people who want real truth.

And spoiler alert: this journey doesn't end in the stars. It ends at a cross—and an empty tomb.

So bring your questions. Your doubts. Your wonder. Your sarcasm. Your faith (or lack of it). There's room for all of it here.

Let's go.

Introduction

What If Faith and Facts Aren't Enemies?

Let's be real for a second.

When you hear the word *faith*, what comes to mind? Church pews? A dusty Bible? A preacher yelling? Or maybe you think of something more personal—your family's beliefs, your own questions, or even your doubts.

Now what about the word *evidence*?

Science. Logic. Cold, hard facts. Something that "smart people" use to disprove religious stuff, right?

That's what a lot of people think: faith and facts are opposites. Faith is what you believe without evidence. Facts are what you know without emotion. You're supposed to pick a side.

But what if that whole idea is wrong?

What if you don't have to choose between your brain and your beliefs? What if faith isn't blind—and what if there's actually solid, honest, logical, real-world *evidence* for why belief in God makes sense?

You shouldn't have to turn off your curiosity to follow Christ. God isn't afraid of science. He invented it. He's not running from your questions. He welcomes them. And you're not alone in asking the big ones, either:

- How did the universe get here?
- Could everything really have come from nothing?
- Why does life feel like it has meaning if we're just random atoms?
- Did Jesus actually live—or was He just made up like a superhero story?
- And if He did live… why does it matter to me right now, in my real life?

These questions don't make you weak. They make you *honest*. And whether you're a doubting believer, a skeptical seeker, or just someone who wants real answers instead of sugar-coated ones, this book is for you.

We'll walk through big ideas, but in a way that makes sense—no PhDs required. You'll learn how science, history, and reason can actually point *toward* God, not away from Him. And most of all, you'll be invited to look at the story that changed the world: the life, death, and resurrection of Jesus.

Not just because it's "what Christians believe," but because it's where all the evidence leads.

This isn't a textbook. It's an invitation.

So flip the page. Read with curiosity. Question boldly. Think deeply. And don't be surprised if, somewhere along the way, God starts to feel closer than you expected.

Part One: The Cosmos

Looking Up—Does the Universe Point to God?

Before we talk about Jesus, we need to zoom way out—like *galaxies-out*.

Every night the stars shine, the planets move, and the laws of physics do their thing without breaking down. The universe is massive, finely tuned, and full of beauty and mystery. But have you ever stopped to ask *why*? Why does any of this even exist? Could it all really come from nothing, on its own, for no reason?

In this section, we're going to explore the big questions that come *before* belief in Jesus:

- Did the Big Bang leave room for God?
- Is the universe just a lucky accident, or was it made on purpose?
- What do math, morality, and meaning tell us about the world we live in?
- And if there's so much pain and evil in the world... does that *disprove* God?

This part isn't about shallow answers or cheesy church slogans. It's about using your brain, engaging with real science and logic, and discovering whether the world you live in points to a personal, intentional Creator.

By the end of this part, you'll be better equipped to answer the question, *"Is it even reasonable to believe in God?"*—and to take the next step: *Who is He?*

Chapter 1

DID THE BIG BANG PROVE GOD EXISTS?

"The more I study science, the more I believe in God."
—*Albert Einstein*

"It's crazy to think the whole universe started from something smaller than a dot."
—*Maya, age 16*

"Science without religion is lame, religion without science is blind."
—*Albert Einstein*

Let's face it: when we start thinking about where the universe came from, it can feel like our brains are about to explode. Stars, galaxies, gravity, time, space, dark matter—what does it all mean? And more importantly, what does it say about God?

You've probably heard of the Big Bang Theory—not the TV show, but the scientific idea that the universe began around 13.8 billion years ago from an unimaginably tiny point and expanded into everything we know today. That includes the sun, your phone, your favorite hoodie, and even you.

Some people say the Big Bang disproves God. Others say it's actually a huge clue that He's real. So, which is it? Let's dig deeper and find out what the evidence actually says—and what that could mean for you.

Boom! And There Was... Everything?

First things first: the Big Bang theory isn't just some random guess—it's backed by decades of research and discovery. In the early 20th century, scientists like Edwin Hubble observed that galaxies are moving away from us, which means the universe is expanding. That's like watching raisin bread rise in the oven—the raisins (galaxies) all move away from each other as the dough (space) expands.

If the universe is expanding, then it must've been smaller in the past. Trace it back far enough, and you get a moment when everything—literally *everything*—was packed into a single, tiny, insanely dense point. Then, in an instant, it expanded. That's the Big Bang.

This idea that the universe had a beginning is where things get really interesting for people of faith.

For centuries, Christians have believed that God created the universe out of nothing. Genesis 1:1 literally starts with, "In the beginning, God created the heavens and the earth." So when scientists started saying, "Hey, it looks like the universe *did* have a beginning," Christians were like, "Well… yeah. We've been saying that all along.

Does a Beginning Mean a Beginner?

Imagine you walk into a room and see a cupcake on the table. It's perfectly frosted with sprinkles on top and a little card that says your name. You wouldn't think, "Wow, that cupcake just randomly appeared out of nowhere." You'd ask, "Who made this?" Because design points to a designer. Beginning points to a beginner.

So if the universe had a beginning, doesn't that mean Someone had to begin it?

In the past, many atheist scientists clung to something called the "steady state" theory. It said that the universe didn't have a beginning—it had always existed. Why? Because if the universe had a beginning, then you'd have to ask questions like: Who started it? What came before? And what kind of being could make something from nothing?

But over time, the evidence for the Big Bang became too strong to ignore. The steady state theory collapsed under the weight of data. The universe had a beginning—and that makes people ask deep, spiritual questions.

Science and Faith: Enemies or Teammates?

Here's something a lot of people get wrong: science and faith are not enemies. They actually make a pretty great team. Science helps us understand *how* things happen. Faith helps us understand *why* things happen.

Think of it like baking cookies. Science tells you how the oven heats the dough and how sugar caramelizes. Faith tells you why your friend made those cookies for you in the first place—because they care. One explains the mechanics, the other gives meaning.

Many of the world's greatest scientists—people like Isaac Newton, Galileo, and Johannes Kepler—believed in God. They didn't think their faith was at odds with science. They believed that studying the universe was a way to get to know the One who created it.

So no, you don't have to choose between science and God. That's a false choice. You can believe in gravity *and* grace. In atoms *and* angels.

What About the Cause?

One of the strongest arguments from the Big Bang for God's existence is something called the "Kalam Cosmological Argument." Don't let the fancy words scare you—it's basically common sense in three simple steps:

1. Whatever begins to exist has a cause.

2. The universe began to exist.
3. Therefore, the universe has a cause.

If the universe had a cause, it must be something outside of the universe. Something timeless, space-less, and super powerful. That sounds a lot like God.

Think about it. Before the Big Bang, there was no time, no space, no matter. So whatever caused the universe had to be beyond all of that. That fits perfectly with how the Bible describes God—eternal, spirit, and all-powerful.

What About Evolution and Other Theories?

Maybe you're thinking, "Okay, but if God used the Big Bang, what about evolution? Or dinosaurs? Or all the other stuff I hear about in science class?"

Great question. The point of this chapter isn't to answer every question (we'll get to more of them later!), but to show that the idea of a beginning doesn't rule out God. In fact, it might point directly to Him.

Some Christians believe God used natural processes like evolution to create life over time. Others believe He created everything more directly and quickly. Either way, the main idea stays the same: the universe had a beginning. And beginnings usually have beginners.

Faith doesn't mean you stop asking questions. Actually, faith *invites* questions. God isn't scared of your curiosity. In fact, your questions might be the very path that leads you closer to Him.

From the Cosmos to You

Here's something wild: the same God who created galaxies, black holes, and quantum physics also created *you*. You're not just cosmic leftovers or stardust that got lucky. You're *fearfully and wonderfully made* (Psalm 139:14). That means your life has value, meaning, and purpose.

The Big Bang might describe the *how*—but only God can tell you the *why*.

Maybe you've looked up at the stars and felt small. That's totally normal. But don't confuse "small" with "insignificant." The God who spoke the universe into existence also speaks love and truth over your life. He knows your name. He wants your heart. And He's closer than you think.

So yes, the Big Bang might be the biggest explosion ever—but it might also be the universe's loudest whisper that you're not alone.

The Takeaway

The Big Bang doesn't disprove God—it might actually be one of the biggest clues pointing to Him. Science and faith aren't enemies;

they're two lenses that help us see reality more clearly. Asking deep questions doesn't make your faith weaker—it can make it stronger. Keep exploring. Keep questioning. Keep seeking. Because the truth will always lead you back to the One who started it all.

Journaling Prompts

1. Have you ever looked at the stars or the night sky and felt curious about where everything came from? What thoughts did that spark in you?

2. What's one thing you've learned about science that made you think more deeply about God?

3. Do you ever feel tension between science and your faith? Why or why not?

4. If the universe had a beginning, what do you think that says about your own purpose?

5. Write a short prayer asking God to help you trust Him more as you seek answers about the world and your place in it.

Chapter 2

WHO MADE GOD?
(AND DOES IT EVEN MATTER?)

"Before the mountains were born or you brought forth the whole world, from everlasting to everlasting you are God."
—*Psalm 90:2*

"Every time I ask where God came from, my brain hurts."
—*Elijah, age 15*

"If there is a God, we are not His equals. We must expect to be puzzled by Him."
—*C.S. Lewis*

There's one question that's bound to come up sooner or later. Maybe you've heard it from a friend, a science video, or even your own thoughts during a late-night spiral: *"Okay, so if God made everything, who made God?"* Boom. Mind blown.

It's a big question—and it's a fair one. In fact, it might be one of the most important questions you ever ask. Not because God has some origin story like a Marvel superhero, but because how you think about God shapes everything else—your identity, your purpose, your hope, and your future.

Let's unpack this together, with honesty, curiosity, and a little help from Scripture, logic, and some everyday illustrations.

Created vs. Uncreated

Here's the deal: everything we know has a cause. Trees come from seeds. Puppies come from other puppies (and their parents, obviously). Even your phone had a beginning—it was designed, built, shipped, and one day it'll stop working (RIP).

So when we say, "Who made God?", we're applying the same logic we use for everything else. But here's the twist—Christians believe that God isn't like everything else.

God isn't created. He's uncreated. He's eternal. He never began, and He'll never end.

Psalm 90:2 says it clearly: "From everlasting to everlasting, You are God." That means God exists outside of time. He didn't "start." He *is*. And while that's hard for our brains to fully grasp, it doesn't make it untrue. It just means God is in a category of His own.

Why Something Has to Be Eternal

Think of a row of dominoes falling. If each domino needed another one to knock it down, you'd eventually ask: who knocked over the first one? You can't have an endless row going backward forever with no first cause. Something had to start the chain.

So if the universe had a beginning (remember the Big Bang from Chapter 1?), something had to cause it—but that cause couldn't itself be caused by anything else. That something must be eternal, powerful, and outside of time and matter.

That's what we mean by "God."

If God were created, then we'd just have to ask, "Well, who created whoever created God?" and we'd be stuck in an endless loop. There has to be an *ultimate* cause—an uncaused cause. And that's who Christians understand God to be.

Doesn't Eternity Sound… Weird?

Let's be honest: the idea of something never beginning is weird. But is it any weirder than the universe suddenly popping into existence for no reason? In fact, most scientists agree that the universe had a starting point. So something had to exist before the universe did. That "something" couldn't be part of the physical universe—it had to be something (or Someone) greater.

Think of it like this: your brain is wired to understand beginnings and endings. We measure everything in time—birthdays, school years, streaming episodes. But God exists outside of time. He invented time. He's not on a timeline like we are. So naturally, trying to box Him into our time-based way of thinking leads to confusion.

But confusion doesn't mean something isn't true. It just means it's bigger than us.

The God Who *Is*

When Moses asked God for His name in Exodus 3, God said: "I AM WHO I AM." That's not a riddle. It's a declaration. God wasn't saying, "I was created by someone else." He was saying, "I exist. Period."

God is the only being whose existence doesn't depend on anything or anyone. He doesn't need food, water, oxygen, or a planet to live on. He just… is. That's what makes Him God.

That's also why God can be trusted. If God were created, He'd be limited. He could change. He might not be all-powerful. But because He's eternal and unchanging, He's the one stable foundation in a world that's always shifting.

So… Does It Matter?

It absolutely matters.

If God had a creator, He wouldn't be God. He'd be just another being in the universe—just another part of the story instead of the author.

But because God is uncreated and eternal, that means:

- He's not fragile. He doesn't wear out. He's always present.
- He's powerful enough to create, sustain, and redeem everything.
- He's worth worshiping, trusting, and following.

And here's the coolest part: this eternal God who always *was*… wants to know *you*.

Eternal Yet Personal

Sometimes we think, "If God is so massive and eternal, why would He care about someone like me?"

But the Bible is full of evidence that God *does* care. In fact, He became a human—Jesus—so we could understand who He is. Jesus, the Son of God, stepped into time and space to show us what love looks like. That's not distant. That's personal.

The eternal God invites you into a relationship that will also last forever. He created you on purpose and for a purpose. You're not a cosmic accident—you're a beloved child.

So yes, it matters deeply that God is uncreated. Because only an eternal God can offer eternal hope.

The Takeaway

Asking "Who made God?" is a natural question, but it misunderstands the nature of who God is. God isn't created—He's eternal. He exists outside of time and space, and He's the uncaused cause of everything. That might stretch your brain (and that's okay!), but it also leads to awe, trust, and a deeper understanding of how big and real God is. Most importantly, the eternal God wants a relationship with you—and that truth changes everything.

Journaling Prompts

1. When you think about God being eternal, what feelings or thoughts come up?

2. Why do you think it's hard for us to imagine something (or Someone) without a beginning?

3. How does knowing God has no beginning or end impact your trust in Him?

4. Read Psalm 90:2 again. What does this verse say to you personally today?

5. Write a prayer asking God to help you trust Him more, even when you don't fully understand His nature.

Chapter 3

DID THE UNIVERSE HAVE A BEGINNING?

"In the beginning God created the heavens and the earth."
— *Genesis 1:1*

"The universe had a beginning. There was once nothing, and now there is something."
— *Dr. William Lane Craig*

"When I look up at the sky, it's wild to think that all of this started somehow. It makes me wonder if there's something—or someone—bigger out there."
— *Layla, age 17*

You've probably had this experience: lying on your back, staring up at a night sky filled with stars, and feeling both really small and really amazed. You wonder, *Where did all this come from? Has it always been here? Did it start at some point—or has it just always existed?* These aren't just science questions. They're heart questions. Because how the universe began—or if it even began—shapes what we believe about life, meaning, and yes, God.

So, did the universe have a beginning? Or has it always existed? Let's dive in.

What Science Actually Says

For centuries, some people believed the universe was eternal—that it had no beginning and had always existed. But that idea began to shift in the 20th century. Scientists like Edwin Hubble discovered that galaxies are moving away from us, which means the universe is expanding. And if it's expanding, that means it had to start from somewhere.

Enter the Big Bang Theory. (No, not the TV show.) It's the leading scientific explanation for how the universe began. According to this theory, the entire universe began from a single point—an unimaginably dense and hot state—and then expanded outward. That first moment, often called the "cosmic beginning," wasn't just the start of matter and energy, but of time and space itself.

Crazy, right? Even more interesting: many scientists were uncomfortable with the idea of a beginning. Not because the evidence wasn't strong, but because a beginning sounds… a lot like a creation. And if there's a creation, it raises the question of a Creator.

The Universe Can't Begin Itself

Here's something to think about: can nothing cause something? If there was absolutely *nothing*—no matter, no energy, no space, no time—could something just pop into existence for no reason?

That's not how anything else works. Your phone didn't just materialize out of nothing. Neither did trees, oceans, or dogs. Everything that begins to exist has a cause.

So if the universe had a beginning, it must have had a cause. And that cause can't be part of the physical universe (because the universe didn't exist yet!). The cause must be outside of time, space, and matter.

That's exactly how the Bible describes God.

Scripture Was There First

Long before telescopes and space probes, the Bible made a bold claim: "In the beginning, God created the heavens and the earth" (Genesis 1:1). The Bible doesn't just say *what* happened—it says *who* made it happen.

This isn't a myth or a poetic idea. It's a foundational truth. God created the universe on purpose and with purpose. Everything we see—the stars, planets, animals, even us—flows from His creative mind.

In Isaiah 45:12, God says, "It is I who made the earth and created mankind upon it. My own hands stretched out the heavens." That's not just beautiful—it lines up with what we now know about the universe having a beginning.

The Fine-Tuning of the Universe

Not only did the universe begin, but it began in an incredibly precise way. Scientists have discovered that many conditions in the universe had to be *exactly right* for life to exist—things like gravity, the strength of electromagnetic forces, and the rate of cosmic expansion.

It's called the "fine-tuning" of the universe, and it's like walking into a room and seeing dozens of knobs and dials all perfectly set. The odds of this happening randomly? Astronomically small.

This fine-tuning doesn't prove God beyond a shadow of a doubt, but it strongly suggests that someone intelligent set the universe up to support life. It looks a lot more like intention than accident.

Why a Beginning Matters

If the universe had a beginning, then it's not eternal. That means it had a starting point—and things with starting points don't usually start themselves. So the idea that the universe had a beginning points us toward something greater than the universe. Something timeless. Something powerful. Something personal.

It's not just about science; it's about worldview. If the universe had a beginning, life isn't random. It's not meaningless. It's part of a bigger story—a story written by the God who began it all.

Jesus affirmed this too. In John 17:5, He talks about the glory He had with the Father *before the world began*. That means even before there was a "when," God already *was*.

But What About Multiverses?

You might have heard of multiverse theories—the idea that there are many (maybe infinite) universes out there. Some people suggest this could explain our universe's beginning and fine-tuning. Maybe, they say, if there are infinite universes, we just happen to be in the lucky one that works.

But there's a catch. Even if there were other universes (and there's no evidence for that yet), the same question applies: *Where did the multiverse come from?* You're still stuck needing a first cause. Infinite copies don't erase the need for an origin.

In the end, even the multiverse idea doesn't solve the beginning problem. It just pushes it back one level. You still need something eternal to kick it all off.

You Were Meant to Begin

Here's where it gets personal: you had a beginning, too. Not just your birth, but your soul, your story, your place in this world. The same God who started the universe also began *you*. He made you with love, and He knows your days from beginning to end (Psalm 139:16).

The universe isn't just a scientific mystery. It's a masterpiece with your name written into it. God started it all—and He hasn't stopped working in it.

The Takeaway

Science and Scripture both point to the same truth: the universe had a beginning. That beginning wasn't random or chaotic—it was intentional. Whether through cosmic background radiation, the expansion of galaxies, or the very fabric of time, creation points to a Creator. A beginning means there's a Beginner. And He isn't just distant—He's present, personal, and pursuing you.

Your life isn't an accident. You're here on purpose. The God who created the stars also created you, and your beginning is just the start of a bigger journey with Him.

Journaling Prompts

1. When you think about the universe having a beginning, what questions or emotions come up?

2. Why do you think some people are uncomfortable with the idea of a Creator?

3. How does Genesis 1:1 change the way you see science and faith?

4. What does it mean to you that the same God who created galaxies also created you?

5. Write a short prayer thanking God for creating you and asking Him to show you more of your purpose.

Chapter 4

SO SATURN IS HOW OLD?
IS INFINITY JUST A BIG LIE?

"When I consider your heavens, the work of your fingers, the moon and the stars, which you have set in place, what is mankind that you are mindful of them?"
— *Psalm 8:3-4*

"It's crazy to think Saturn's rings are older than humanity. I mean, how do you even measure something that big?"
— *Jordan, age 16*

"Infinity is bigger than the biggest number you can think of. But does that make it real?"
— *A math teacher on TikTok*

Time. We all live in it, but we barely understand it. You have 24 hours in a day (unless you're on Mercury, where a single day is longer than a year—look it up!). You get older, your phone gets outdated, and your pizza gets cold. But time isn't just about clocks ticking and calendars flipping. It's deeply tied to the way we understand the universe—and God.

When people ask how old the Earth is, or how long the stars have been burning, they're asking time questions. And time is one of those topics where science, faith, and philosophy collide in fascinating—and sometimes confusing—ways.

So let's talk about Saturn, age, infinity, and what it all tells us about God.

Saturn's Rings and Cosmic Clocks

Scientists estimate Saturn is over 4.5 billion years old. That's a massive number—like, mind-bendingly huge. Its rings, though, might be much younger. Some studies suggest they formed "only" a few hundred million years ago. Still older than anything on Earth except rocks, but a baby in cosmic terms.

How do scientists figure this stuff out? They study light, gravity, motion, and radioactive decay. It's like detective work on a galactic scale. And while we might not agree on every detail of how old the universe is, Christians and scientists can both agree that the universe is *finely tuned*, *awe-inspiring*, and *not eternal*.

Saturn, with its rings that glow in sunlight like cosmic jewelry, reminds us that beauty takes time—and that time itself had a starting point. Just like the universe.

Can Something Be Infinite?

You've probably heard the word "infinity" thrown around. Infinite loops. Infinite scroll. Infinite fries (we wish). It sounds cool, but is infinity actually real? Or is it just a human idea for something we can't count?

In math, infinity is used as a concept. But in the real world, we've never seen anything that's *actually infinite*. Even the universe—no matter how vast—isn't proven to be infinite. And time? It sure seems to move forward, second by second, from a beginning point.

Philosopher William Lane Craig argues that actual infinities can't exist in reality. Imagine trying to count backward through an infinite number of days to get to today. You'd never get here. That's why most philosophers and scientists agree: time had a beginning. And if it had a beginning, something had to *start* it.

So while "infinity" might be cool in theory, it doesn't explain the real world very well. It points to the need for something *beyond* numbers—something eternal, but not infinite in the same way.

God: Eternal, Not Infinite in Time

God doesn't live in time the way we do. He's not stuck on a clock or waiting for next Tuesday. He is eternal—not infinite *in time*, but *outside of time*.

The Bible describes God as "the Alpha and the Omega" (Revelation 1:8), meaning the beginning and the end. In Psalm 90:2, it says, "Before the mountains were born or you brought forth the whole world, from everlasting to everlasting you are God."

That's wild. God doesn't just live *a long time*. He created time. That means He was never "young" and will never "get old." He sees the end from the beginning and exists fully in every moment. That's hard to wrap our heads around—but it's also incredibly comforting. It means God is never late, never confused, and always aware of what we need—even before we ask.

The Problem with an Eternal Universe

Some people want the universe to be eternal, stretching back forever. That way, they think, we don't need a beginning—or a Beginner. But the more we learn, the more that idea falls apart.

As we saw in Chapter 3, the universe is expanding, cooling down, and running out of usable energy. That process, called "entropy," means the universe is wearing out like an old hoodie. That's not what you'd expect from something that's always been around.

And remember: if time never had a start, you could never reach this moment. It would be like trying to climb out of a bottomless pit—you'd never get here. So if we're *here*, that's evidence that time—and the universe—had a beginning.

So Why Does This Matter?

All this talk about time, infinity, and Saturn's age isn't just brainy science stuff. It has soul-level implications. Because if time had a beginning, it means history is going somewhere. It means your life is part of a story. It means you weren't dropped randomly into a chaotic universe. You were *placed* here, in this time, on purpose.

That's what Acts 17:26–27 says: "He marked out their appointed times in history and the boundaries of their lands. God did this so that they would seek him." God knows the timing of your life. He picked your generation, your friend group, your challenges, and your gifts—not by accident, but with intention.

Living in Time with an Eternal God

God made time, and He made you. And even though you live in time—with school schedules, birthdays, and deadlines—God invites you to live connected to eternity.

In John 17:3, Jesus says, "Now this is eternal life: that they know you, the only true God, and Jesus Christ, whom you have sent." Eternal life doesn't just start after you die. It starts the moment you know God. It's about living in relationship with the One who is outside time but chose to step into it—for you.

That's what Jesus did. He entered time. He was born in a specific year, in a small town, with a human body and a human clock. He did it so He could walk with us, die for us, and rise to give us life that *never ends*.

The Takeaway

Infinity might be a cool math concept, but it doesn't explain the real world we live in. Time had a beginning. The universe had a starting point. And God—eternal and outside of time—created both. That means your life is not random or meaningless. You were created for a time such as this, to know the God who exists beyond numbers, years, and galaxies. He holds Saturn in His hand—and He holds you, too.

Journaling Prompts

1. What do you feel when you think about the age of the universe or planets like Saturn?

2. Why do you think God created time instead of making everything happen all at once?

3. How does knowing God is eternal (outside of time) give you peace in your daily life?

4. What's one way you can "live eternally" today by focusing on what really matters?

5. Write a short prayer thanking God for placing you in *this* time and asking Him to help you use it well.

Chapter 5

IS THE UNIVERSE A GIANT COINCIDENCE... OR DID SOMEONE DESIGN IT FOR US?

"The heavens declare the glory of God; the skies proclaim the work of his hands."
— *Psalm 19:1*

"You know when something's just *too* perfect to be random? Like, there has to be a designer behind it."
— *Ava, 17*

"I cannot imagine how the clockwork of the universe can exist without a clockmaker."
— *Voltaire*

Ever stared up at the stars and thought, "Wow, that can't just be a coincidence"? Maybe it was a clear night, and the stars stretched like glitter across a dark canvas. Or maybe you've heard how finely tuned our universe is and wondered, "How could this possibly all happen by chance?"

You're not alone. People—scientists, artists, teenagers, philosophers—have asked these same questions for thousands of years. Because the more we learn about the universe, the more it looks like everything had to be *just right* for us to exist. Like someone planned it. Like someone *wanted* us here.

So is the universe just a lucky accident, or is there evidence of design? And if there is, what does that mean for your life and faith?

The Fine-Tuned Universe

Let's talk about fine-tuning. No, not like tuning a guitar (though that's cool, too). Fine-tuning means the universe operates within incredibly specific settings—almost like dials on a control panel—that had to be precisely calibrated or life wouldn't be possible.

Here's what we mean. If gravity were slightly stronger or weaker, stars couldn't form. If the strength of the strong nuclear force (which holds atoms together) was just a little off, matter itself wouldn't exist. If the rate of expansion after the Big Bang had been just a tiny bit faster or slower, the universe would've either collapsed or expanded too fast for galaxies to form.

And get this: the odds of all these settings landing in the right place by chance are ridiculously small. Like, smaller than winning the lottery every day for a year. That's why many scientists—even nonreligious ones—have said it *looks* like the universe was designed.

Is Chance a Good Enough Explanation?

Some people say, "Well, maybe we just got lucky." Kind of like winning a cosmic Powerball. But here's the thing: luck isn't an explanation. It's what you say when you *don't* have one.

Imagine walking into a room and seeing your name spelled out in Scrabble tiles on the floor. Would you think, "Wow, those just randomly fell that way"? Or would you look for who did it? The more specific and meaningful something is, the harder it is to chalk it up to chance.

The universe isn't just random. It's full of order, beauty, and purpose. From DNA's tiny coded instructions in your cells to the massive laws that govern galaxies, it all points to a deeper meaning. And chance just doesn't explain that kind of intentionality.

The Watchmaker and the Blueprint

Back in the 1700s, a guy named William Paley came up with an illustration that's still used today. He said if you found a watch on the ground, you wouldn't assume it just appeared out of nowhere. You'd know it was made by someone—because watches are complex and serve a purpose.

Paley argued the same is true for the universe. If it's full of design, there must be a *Designer*.

Today we know way more than Paley did, and the case for design has only gotten stronger. Take DNA, for example. It's basically a language written inside every living thing. Languages don't happen by accident. Codes come from minds. The more we discover, the more fingerprints we see. And those fingerprints point to God.

What the Bible Says About Creation

Long before modern science, Scripture already told us that creation points to God. Psalm 19:1 says, "The heavens declare the glory of God." Romans 1:20 adds, "For since the creation of the world God's invisible qualities—his eternal power and divine nature—have been clearly seen, being understood from what has been made."

God's Word tells us something we feel deep down when we look at nature: it wasn't random. It was made by someone powerful, creative, and personal. And that Someone made it not just for fun—but for *you* to know Him.

Isaiah 45:18 puts it plainly: "For this is what the Lord says—he who created the heavens, he is God; he who fashioned and made the earth, he founded it; he did not create it to be empty, but formed it to be inhabited." God made this world with purpose and design, and you're part of that design.

But What About Evolution and Science?

Some teens wonder: "If I believe in science, can I still believe in God?" The answer is a confident *yes*. Science and faith aren't enemies—they're friends.

Science asks, "How does this work?" Faith asks, "Why is it here?"

Believing that God designed the universe doesn't mean you ignore science. In fact, many scientists believe in God *because* of what they discover. Whether you believe God created life all at once or used processes over time, the point is: God is the *why* behind the *how*. And His fingerprints are everywhere.

You're Not a Cosmic Accident

Here's where it gets personal. If the universe was designed, then your life isn't random. You're not a meaningless speck on a pale blue dot. You are part of a grand design. And your story matters to the One who wrote it.

Ephesians 2:10 says, "We are God's handiwork, created in Christ Jesus to do good works, which God prepared in advance for us to do." You are God's creation. His masterpiece. His intentional design.

That changes everything. Because if your life has design, it also has direction. You're not floating in space without a map. You're walking with the One who made the stars—and made *you*, too.

The Takeaway

The more we discover about the universe, the less it looks like a coincidence. From the fine-tuning of physical laws to the complexity of DNA, creation points to a Creator. The Bible affirms what science suggests: the universe is designed. And you—right here, right now—are part of that design. You're not an accident. You're an image-bearer of the God who made everything and calls it good.

Journaling Prompts

1. What's one part of creation that makes you feel closest to God? Why?

2. Do you think it's harder or easier to believe in God when you learn more about science? Why?

3. How does it feel to know that your life isn't a coincidence?

4. What's something in nature or space that you find amazing? What might it show you about God?

5. Write a prayer thanking God for the beauty and order in creation—and for creating you with purpose.

Chapter 6

IF MATH IS A LANGUAGE, WHO'S SPEAKING?

"Mathematics is the language in which God has written the universe."
— *Galileo Galilei*

"Math is like a code. It's hard, but when it clicks, everything makes sense."
— *Maya, age 15*

"In the beginning was the Word, and the Word was with God, and the Word was God."
— *John 1:1*

Have you ever sat in math class and thought, *Why do I need to know this?* You're not alone. For many teens, math feels like a never-ending stream of formulas, equations, and strange symbols. But what if math is more than just a school subject? What if it's a *language*—a way of understanding and describing the world? And even more, what if that language is a clue that someone is trying to communicate with us?

The more you dig into math—not just homework problems but the deep stuff—the more you find something oddly beautiful. Fractals. Fibonacci sequences. Pi. Patterns in the stars, the petals of a flower, the shells on the beach. It's like someone left fingerprints in every corner of creation. But who?

Let's dive into the idea that math is a language—and explore who might be the One speaking it.

Math: The Universal Translator

Here's something wild: math works *everywhere*. Whether you're in Los Angeles or on Mars, 2 + 2 is still 4. Gravity obeys formulas. Planets move in precise orbits. Buildings stand tall because engineers rely on geometric truths that always hold. Math is like a code that translates across cultures, languages, and even galaxies.

That consistency has puzzled and inspired scientists for centuries. Why does the universe behave in a logical, ordered, and *understandable* way? The famous physicist Eugene Wigner called this the "unreasonable effectiveness of mathematics." In other words, it's weird—and amazing—that math works so perfectly in describing nature.

It's almost like the universe was *meant* to be understood. Like someone built it with logic, structure, and purpose.

Could It All Be Random?

Some people believe the universe just *happened*—no design, no plan, just randomness. But math doesn't look random. Think about it: randomness doesn't lead to repeating patterns, symmetries, or precise constants like the speed of light or the gravitational pull of Earth.

In fact, the deeper scientists go, the more they rely on mathematical truths to discover the next layer of reality. Even the Big Bang theory—the idea that the universe had a beginning—depends on mathematical models. If the universe came from chaos, how did order emerge? How did math emerge? Isn't it strange that something so abstract and immaterial could shape something so physical and real?

That's where God enters the conversation. If math is a language, maybe it exists because a rational, intelligent Being *spoke* it into existence.

God: The Divine Mathematician

The Bible doesn't say "God is a calculator." But it does say He is a God of order, wisdom, and design. Look at Proverbs 3:19: "By wisdom the Lord laid the earth's foundations, by understanding he set the heavens in place." That's poetic language—but it's also profoundly logical. God used wisdom, knowledge, and intentionality to create everything.

And John 1:1 calls Jesus the "Word"—in Greek, *Logos*, which also means reason, order, or logic. In other words, Jesus is the divine reason behind everything that exists. That's why the patterns we see in math and science don't just point to some kind of order—they point to *Someone*. Not just a principle, but a person.

Think about this: If you found a book full of perfect code, your first assumption wouldn't be that it wrote itself. You'd wonder who the author was. The universe is that book. Math is the ink. God is the Author.

Created to Understand

One of the most amazing things about humans is that we can *do* math. We can understand equations, solve problems, and use logic. Animals can't do algebra. Rocks don't understand fractions. But we can.

Why? Genesis 1:27 gives us the answer: "God created mankind in his own image." That means we are designed to reflect God in some way—including our ability to think logically, solve problems, and explore creation. Our brains are wired to understand the world He made, because He made us to know Him.

That's why learning—even when it's hard—is an act of worship. When you wrestle with a tough problem, when you finally understand a complicated idea, you're not just passing a test. You're using a gift God gave you to uncover the structure of His creation.

The Language of Worship

There's another side to this, too. The more we understand the language of math and science, the more we can stand in awe of the One who designed it all. That awe can lead us to worship.

Psalm 19:1 says, "The heavens declare the glory of God; the skies proclaim the work of his hands." They don't speak in words—but they do speak in math. In the harmony of their motion. In the laws that govern their paths. In the very fact that we can write formulas to describe the orbit of Saturn or the shape of a raindrop.

Worship isn't just singing songs—it's recognizing God's greatness and responding with your whole life. And when you understand that God speaks through math, suddenly that geometry class or chemistry lab becomes holy ground.

More Than Logic

But let's not stop at logic. God is not *just* logical. He is also love. The same God who wrote the equations for the galaxies also counts the hairs on your head (Luke 12:7). He knows you personally. That means the One who speaks the language of math also speaks the language of your heart.

And through Jesus, He's inviting you into a relationship. Not just to *study* Him like a subject, but to *know* Him like a friend. To trust Him. To love Him. To live for Him.

The Takeaway

Math is more than numbers—it's a language. A language that reveals patterns, structure, and beauty in creation. And every language has a speaker. In the case of math, that speaker is God—the eternal Creator who designed the universe with precision and purpose. You were made in His image to understand that language, to explore His creation, and to reflect His wisdom. And ultimately, math isn't just about solving equations. It's about hearing the voice of the One who made you—and learning to trust Him with everything.

Journaling Prompts

1. Have you ever seen something in nature that made you feel like it was designed on purpose? What was it?

2. How do you feel about math? Has this chapter changed the way you think about it?

3. What does it mean to you that you're made in the image of a logical, creative God?

4. In what areas of your life do you see God's order and design?

5. Write a short prayer asking God to help you see His presence even in subjects or situations that feel difficult or confusing.

Chapter 7

WHY IS THERE SOMETHING RATHER THAN NOTHING?

"The most incomprehensible thing about the universe is that it is comprehensible."
— *Albert Einstein*

"Sometimes I wonder why anything exists at all. Like... why not just *nothing* forever?"
— *Caleb, age 16*

"By faith we understand that the universe was formed at God's command, so that what is seen was not made out of what was visible."
— *Hebrews 11:3*

Have you ever looked up at the stars and just...paused? Maybe you were lying on a trampoline, or walking home at night, or just had one of those moments where the universe felt really *big*. And for a second, you thought: *Why is all of this here?* Why is there a universe? A planet? Trees, music, laughter, math, gravity...you?

That's not just a question for science class. It's one of the deepest, oldest questions humans have ever asked: Why is there something rather than nothing?

It's a question that cuts through all the noise. It's the beginning of wonder. And even though you might not get a full answer in one sitting, this chapter is here to help you walk toward the truth—one step at a time, with honesty, humility, and hope.

The Problem With Nothing

Let's start by imagining *nothing*. Not empty space—not a vacuum or darkness. Just…nothing. No atoms, no space, no time, no ideas, no math, no God, no anything. Can you even picture it? Probably not. That's because our minds are made for *something*. We live in a world of cause and effect, where things happen because something made them happen. We take for granted that things exist.

But the question still stands: Why do they? Why should there be *anything* at all?

Some scientists and philosophers have tried to say that the universe just popped into being. That it came out of nothing. But when you dig a little deeper, "nothing" often turns out to be *something*—a quantum vacuum, or fluctuating fields, or mathematical laws. In other words, not truly nothing. And that still doesn't answer why those things were there in the first place.

If we keep pushing the question back far enough, we eventually hit a wall: either something has always existed, or there was once *nothing*, and somehow, something came out of it. One of those makes more sense—and it's not the one that starts with nothing.

A Necessary Being

Philosophers have a name for what the universe needs: a *necessary being*. Something that didn't come from anything else. Something that has always existed and doesn't depend on anything outside of itself. A being like that could explain why anything exists at all.

That's where the Christian view of God comes in. The Bible says God is eternal (Psalm 90:2). He wasn't created. He just *is*. When Moses asked God what His name was, God replied, "I AM WHO I AM" (Exodus 3:14). That's not just poetic. It's deep. It means God's existence isn't borrowed or temporary. He exists necessarily. Always has, always will.

If God exists necessarily, then He's not just an answer to the question, "Why something instead of nothing?" He's *the* answer.

Did God Create Because He Needed To?

Sometimes people ask, "If God always existed, why did He create anything?" Was He bored? Lonely? Did He need us?

The Bible tells us that God is complete in Himself. He didn't create out of loneliness but out of *love*. God exists as a Trinity—Father, Son, and Holy Spirit—meaning relationship, love, and joy existed within God before anything was made. Creation wasn't about filling a gap in God's heart. It was about sharing His goodness with others.

Like an artist painting a canvas not because they have to, but because beauty wants to be expressed. God created out of overflow—not out of lack.

Something Points to Someone

Everything that exists carries clues about its origin. The complexity of DNA, the fine-tuning of the universe, the laws of physics—all these suggest intentionality. But beyond the science, there's something even more personal: your own existence.

You didn't choose to be born. You didn't set the laws of physics that keep you breathing. Your very life is a gift you didn't earn. That raises an even more intimate question: *What am I here for?*

If there's a God who created everything, including you, then your life isn't an accident. You're not a random collection of atoms. You're part of a story. And God is the Author.

The Empty Throne

When people try to explain existence without God, they often end up replacing Him with something else—energy, multiverses, chance, even math. But none of those things can choose, love, or give meaning. They're descriptions of what exists, not explanations for why anything exists at all.

Imagine a throne sitting in the center of the universe. If God isn't sitting on it, something else will be. But whatever you put there has to answer the biggest questions of existence. If it can't, it doesn't belong there.

Only God is big enough, eternal enough, and personal enough to sit on that throne.

Faith That Thinks

Hebrews 11:3 reminds us that by faith we understand that the universe was made by God. But this isn't blind faith. It's faith that *thinks*. Faith that explores. Faith that isn't afraid of hard questions because it knows that truth isn't fragile.

Christianity doesn't shut down big questions. It invites them. God's not intimidated by your doubts. He's bigger than all of them—and He's closer than you think.

So if you've ever asked, "Why is there something rather than nothing?"—good. That's the kind of question that leads to worship.

To humility. To truth. And ultimately, to the God who not only *made* everything, but who *wants* to be known by you.

The Takeaway

The question "Why is there something rather than nothing?" is more than philosophical—it's personal. It leads us to consider the kind of Being who could explain all existence: one who is eternal, self-existent, powerful, and loving. The Bible reveals that Being to be God. Not only did He create the universe, but He created *you*—with purpose, value, and meaning. You're here not by accident, but because a loving God decided that the world needed *you* in it.

Journaling Prompts

1. Have you ever thought about the question, "Why is there something rather than nothing?" What emotions come up when you do?

2. How does the idea of God as a "necessary being" shape the way you think about creation?

3. What does it mean to you that God created out of love and not out of need?

4. In what ways have you seen or felt the evidence of God's intentionality in your own life?

5. Write a prayer thanking God for creating you and inviting Him to help you understand your purpose in His story.

Chapter 8

CAN YOU BE GOOD WITHOUT GOD?

"If God does not exist, everything is permitted."
— *Fyodor Dostoevsky*

"People say you don't need religion to be a good person. But what do we even mean by 'good'?"
— *Sydney, age 17*

"There is no one righteous, not even one... there is no one who does good, not even one."
— *Romans 3:10, 12*

What do we mean by "good"? It's a question that's probably come up in your brain or in a conversation at some point—maybe even in a heated debate: *"You don't need God to be a good person."* And honestly, it can sound pretty convincing. After all, plenty of people who don't believe in God are kind, generous, and loving. They donate to charity, help their neighbors, and stand up for justice. So... case closed?

Not quite. Let's press pause and back up. What do we even mean when we say "good"? Are we talking about following rules? Being nice? Doing more good things than bad ones? And if that's the case, who gets to decide what counts as "good"? This is where things get real. Because to answer whether we can be good without God, we first have to ask: *What is good, and where does that idea come from?*

The Problem with Relative Morality

Imagine you're playing a game of soccer, but no one agrees on the rules. One person says you can use your hands. Another says there are no fouls. Someone else says the goals don't matter. It would be chaos. You'd argue over every call because there's no agreed-upon standard.

That's what happens when we try to define goodness without a moral standard. If there's no God, then who or what defines right and wrong? Society? Culture? Personal feelings? All of those things change. What one culture says is right, another might say is wrong. What feels good today might not feel good tomorrow.

Without God, morality becomes relative—like a game with no clear rules. That might sound freeing at first, but eventually, it leads to confusion, injustice, and even despair. Because if there's no ultimate good, then evil becomes just another opinion.

A Moral Law Means a Moral Lawgiver

In his book *Mere Christianity*, C.S. Lewis pointed out that we all argue about right and wrong, like people fighting over a seat on the bus: "That's my seat—you took it!" But here's the thing: we don't argue unless we believe there's a real standard that's been violated.

Even kids know when something's unfair. When someone cheats, steals, or lies, we feel the injustice deep down. That points to something bigger—what Lewis called the "Moral Law." And just like a law needs a lawgiver, a moral law points to a moral lawgiver.

God isn't just a rulemaker—He *is* goodness. His nature defines what is good. Kindness, justice, truth, mercy—those are reflections of *who God is*. So if we want to understand what's truly good, we have to start with Him.

Can Atheists Be Good?

This might surprise you: yes, atheists can do good things. That's not up for debate. The Bible even acknowledges that people who don't follow God can still act in ways that align with God's moral design (see Romans 2:14-15). That's because God wired His moral law into every human heart. Whether we admit it or not, we all have a conscience—a compass that points us toward right and wrong.

But here's the deeper point: while you can do good *without believing* in God, there wouldn't *be* good at all if God didn't exist. In other words, you can live in God's world, benefit from His design, and even reflect His character without acknowledging Him. But that doesn't mean the goodness comes from you—it ultimately comes from Him.

It's like using sunlight to grow a plant while denying the sun exists. You're still using the light, but you're ignoring the source.

Broken Goodness

Another part of the story is that none of us are completely good. We all mess up—sometimes in small ways, sometimes in huge ones. The Bible puts it bluntly: "There is no one who does good, not even one" (Romans 3:12). That's not meant to shame us, but to open our eyes to the truth: we need help.

Being "good enough" isn't the goal. And in God's eyes, it's not even possible. That's because God is perfectly holy. His standard isn't "better than average"—it's moral perfection. If we're honest, we all fall short.

That's why Jesus matters. He didn't just come to teach goodness. He came to *be* our goodness. Through Him, we can be made right with God—not because of what we've done, but because of what He did for us on the cross.

Why It Matters

So back to the big question: Can you be good without God?

If we mean "Can you do nice things and help people?"—sure. People do that every day. But if we mean "Can you define, ground, and live out moral goodness in a way that makes sense of the universe?"—then no. Because without God, morality loses its foundation.

If goodness is real—and most of us live like it is—then it must be rooted in something bigger than us. God's existence isn't just a religious claim; it's the best explanation for why things like love, justice, and truth matter so much. Without Him, they're just feelings. With Him, they're eternal.

What About You?

Maybe you've tried to "be a good person" and still felt empty. Or maybe you've made mistakes and feel like you're too far gone. Here's the hope: God isn't asking you to earn your way into His love. He's inviting you to *receive* it.

Real goodness begins not with effort, but with grace. When you let Jesus in, He doesn't just make you better—He makes you *new*. And from that new heart flows a new kind of goodness. Not one based on fear or performance, but one rooted in love.

The Takeaway

You can do good things without believing in God, but goodness itself doesn't make sense without Him. Morality needs a foundation—one that doesn't change with culture or opinion. The Bible reveals God not just as a rulemaker, but as the very definition of goodness. Through Jesus, we're not only shown what goodness looks like—we're given a new heart to live it out. Being "good" isn't about perfection. It's about knowing the One who is good and letting Him shape your life.

Journaling Prompts

1. What do you think makes something "good" or "bad"? Where did those ideas come from?

2. Have you ever felt pressure to be "good enough"? How does grace challenge or encourage that mindset?

3. In what ways have you seen God's goodness reflected in people around you?

4. What's the difference between doing good things and becoming a good person in God's eyes?

5. Write a prayer asking God to help you understand His goodness and live it out with His help.

Chapter 9

Could God Be Like...A Pizza?

"The fool says in his heart, 'There is no God.'"
— *Psalm 14:1*

"God is not just an idea we wish were true. He's the reason we can even have ideas at all."
— *Marcus, age 18*

"God said to Moses, 'I AM WHO I AM.'"
— *Exodus 3:14*

Okay, let's start weird. Have you ever sat around with friends and said something totally out there like, *"What if God was like...a pizza?"* It sounds ridiculous, but roll with it for a second. You've got your crust (the base), your sauce (adds flavor), cheese (essential), and toppings (all the extra stuff people fight over). Each part adds something, but none of them are the whole pizza on their own. Now imagine someone saying, "This pizza is *the best* possible pizza." Like, no other pizza could ever be better.

What if we took that idea and applied it to God—not to say He's edible or cheesy—but to explore something deep: what it means for something (or Someone) to be the *greatest conceivable being*. That's exactly what a guy named Anselm tried to do over 900 years ago. And he kicked off a conversation that still blows minds today. It's called the **ontological argument**. Don't worry, we'll unpack it in plain English. No philosophy degree required.

The Greatest Being Possible

So, let's break it down. Anselm said that God is "that than which nothing greater can be conceived." Translation? God is the greatest being your brain can imagine. Like, the top of the top. If you can imagine something greater, then *that* would be God.

Now here's where it gets wild. Anselm argued that if the greatest possible being exists *only* in your imagination and *not* in reality, then it's not actually the greatest. Because something that exists in real life is better than something that's just a thought. A perfect friend in your mind is cool—but a real friend who's actually there for you? Way better.

So if God is the greatest being we can possibly imagine, then He can't just exist in your mind—He *must* exist in reality too. Otherwise, He wouldn't be the greatest possible being. Mind = blown.

But Wait…Is That Even Logical?

You might be thinking, *"Hold on—can you just define something into existence? Can I say, 'I imagine the greatest pizza ever and therefore it must exist?'"* That's a fair question.

The key difference is that pizza isn't a necessary being. You can imagine a really good pizza, but it's still made of stuff—dough, sauce, cheese. It could exist or not exist, and the universe would go on. But if there is a being that must exist in order for *anything* else to exist—something that's not made, not limited, not dependent—then that being would have to exist by nature. That's the idea behind God in the ontological argument.

God isn't like other things. He's not one pizza among many. He's the chef, the oven, the recipe, the inventor of flavor itself. You can't imagine a world where pizza never existed until someone made it. But try to imagine a world where God didn't exist at all. In that world, not even the rules of logic would exist—because God is the foundation for *everything.*

God Is Necessary, Not Optional

This is where it really matters. God is what philosophers call a "necessary being"—He can't *not* exist. He's not just one being in the universe. He's the reason the universe exists in the first place. Unlike everything else that needs a cause, a source, or an explanation, God simply *is*. That's why in Exodus 3:14, God says, "I AM WHO I AM."

That name means more than just "I exist." It means "I exist necessarily. I don't depend on anything. I'm the source of all that is."

This is important because it's not just a mental exercise—it's about trust. If God exists necessarily, then so does His love, His justice, and His promises. You don't have to wonder if He's going to ghost you one day or disappear when life gets hard. He's not like us. He doesn't change. He's not a trend. He's *real*, eternal, and unshakable.

Your Thoughts Can't Create God

One of the mind-bending parts of the ontological argument is this: the idea of God isn't something humans invented. It's something our minds *receive*—like a signal we didn't send but can't ignore. Why? Because we were made in His image (Genesis 1:27). We are wired to long for what's perfect, eternal, loving, and just. We didn't make up those things—they're echoes of the God who *is*.

And here's something even crazier: the fact that we can even ask questions like "Does God exist?" points to a deeper truth. We have minds that can think abstractly, hearts that long for meaning, and souls that ache for more than survival. If we were just random atoms bouncing around, why would we care about truth, beauty, justice—or even pizza?

From Argument to Worship

Arguments like the ontological one can sound like logic puzzles. But at the heart of it is something sacred. It's not just about proving God exists. It's about being blown away by *who* He is.

God isn't just a being among other beings. He's being itself. The Source. The Origin. The Reason anything exists at all. And that means we're not accidents. You're not random. Your longing for something more is not weakness—it's your soul waking up to reality.

When you realize that the greatest possible Being exists—not just in thought but in truth—it doesn't end in a debate. It leads to awe. Worship. Surrender. Because this God who must exist is also the God who chose to love, rescue, and invite *you* into His life.

The Takeaway

The ontological argument shows us something powerful: if God is the greatest being we can possibly imagine, then He must exist—not just in our thoughts, but in reality. Unlike pizza, which is delicious but optional, God is necessary. He's not created or dependent. He *is*. And that changes everything. Because this necessary, eternal God has revealed Himself—not only through philosophy or logic, but through Scripture, through creation, and most personally, through Jesus. He's not just a theory—He's the truth behind all things.

Journaling Prompts

1. Have you ever imagined what the "greatest being" would be like? What qualities would that being have?

2. How does the idea that God is "necessary" (not optional) affect the way you think about Him?

3. What's the difference between knowing about God in your mind and knowing Him in your heart?

4. Have you ever doubted God's existence? What made you question—and what helps restore your trust?

5. Write a prayer of awe, worship, or curiosity about God's nature. Ask Him to show you more of who He truly is.

Chapter 10

CAN EVIL AND SUFFERING REALLY CANCEL OUT GOD?

> "If God is all-powerful and loving, why is there so much pain in the world?"
> — *Ava, age 16*

> "God whispers to us in our pleasures, speaks in our conscience, but shouts in our pain."
> — *C.S. Lewis*

> "Even though I walk through the valley of the shadow of death, I will fear no evil, for you are with me..."
> — *Psalm 23:4*

Let's be real: if there's one thing that makes people question God more than anything else, it's suffering. Maybe you've lost someone you loved. Maybe someone betrayed you, or you've seen stories of war, injustice, or natural disasters that shake your heart. You wonder: *If God is real, and if He's good, how could He possibly let this happen?*

You're not alone. Everyone from ancient philosophers to TikTok teens has wrestled with this. It's called "the problem of evil," and it's one of the biggest arguments people use to challenge the existence of God. But here's the thing—it's not just an intellectual problem. It's personal. When you're hurting, explanations don't always help. What you want is comfort, healing, hope.

This chapter won't solve every mystery of suffering, but it *will* help you think clearly and honestly about it. And more than that, it will show how even in the deepest pain, God is not absent. In fact, He may be closer than ever.

Does Evil Prove God Isn't Real?

At first glance, it seems like suffering is strong evidence against God. If He's all-powerful, He *could* stop evil. If He's loving, He *would* want to. So why doesn't He? That's the tension.

But let's flip the question: where do we even get the idea that evil is wrong? If we're just random molecules bumping around, if the universe is just time + matter + chance, why would anything like injustice, cruelty, or pain even *matter*? Yet deep down, we all know that things like murder, abuse, and racism are *wrong*. Not just personally inconvenient—actually wrong.

And that's the clue. The moment we call something evil, we're assuming a moral standard—something that says, "This should not be." And moral standards don't come from nature. They come from a mind. From a Person. From God.

Ironically, the very argument that suffering disproves God actually points us back to Him. The more you feel that the world *ought* to be better, the more you're echoing God's heart—and revealing that you were made in His image.

God Didn't Create Evil—But He Allowed Choice

Genesis chapter 1 tells us that God made everything "very good." No sickness, no death, no tears. So what happened?

God created humans with free will—the ability to choose love, truth, and goodness, or to walk away from it. Why? Because love isn't real if it's forced. Robots can be programmed to say "I love you," but it's not meaningful unless it's chosen.

Tragically, humanity chose rebellion. And that choice brought in suffering, death, and brokenness—not just spiritually, but physically and emotionally. We live in the fallout of that decision. We still bear God's image, but it's been fractured by sin. That's why there's cancer, war, and loneliness. This world isn't how it was meant to be.

God didn't create evil, but He gave us the freedom to choose—and in that freedom, pain entered the story. But that's not the end.

God Steps into the Suffering

Here's the radical difference between Christianity and every other worldview: God doesn't stay distant from our pain. He *enters* it.

In Jesus, God stepped into our broken world—not as a king in a castle, but as a baby born into poverty, pain, and persecution. He faced betrayal, abuse, injustice, hunger, and grief. He didn't just *see* our suffering—He *felt* it.

And on the cross, Jesus took the full weight of evil on Himself. The worst injustice in history happened to the only truly innocent person. But through that suffering, He defeated sin and made a way for healing, hope, and eternal life. The cross doesn't remove our questions, but it shows us that God isn't indifferent—He cares enough to bleed.

Why Doesn't He Stop It Now?

If God is going to end evil, why doesn't He just do it already?

Short answer: He will. But He's waiting—not because He's weak, but because He's patient. 2 Peter 3:9 says God is "not slow… but patient, not wanting anyone to perish." If He wiped out all evil *right now*, He'd have to wipe out *us*, too. Because evil isn't just "out there"—it's in every heart.

Instead, He offers mercy. A chance to repent. A chance to change. A chance to come home. And in the meantime, He works *through* suffering, not just around it. He brings beauty out of ashes. He heals what was shattered. And one day, Revelation 21:4 promises that He will "wipe away every tear… there will be no more death or mourning or crying or pain."

We live in the in-between—the "already but not yet." Jesus has defeated sin, but we still wait for the day He fully restores all things. Until then, we don't suffer alone.

Suffering Can Actually Strengthen Faith

It sounds backward, but some of the strongest believers have been through the deepest pain. Why? Because in suffering, you realize how weak everything else is. Money, popularity, success—none of it lasts. But God does.

Romans 5:3-5 says that suffering produces perseverance, character, and hope. That's not just poetry—it's real. Pain can either crush you or carve you. When you lean into God, He meets you there. He gives you peace that doesn't make sense, strength you didn't think you had, and purpose even in the darkest nights.

What About the People Who Never Find Relief?

This is the part that hurts the most. What about the people who suffer for years—who die from hunger, disease, or abuse without ever seeing justice or healing?

We grieve those stories. We cry over them. And so does God. But the Bible tells us this life isn't the end of the story. There is a just Judge. There is a final day. There is an eternal hope for those who trust in Jesus.

The promise of Christianity isn't that we'll be spared from suffering—it's that suffering doesn't win. Jesus rose from the dead. That changes everything. It means evil doesn't get the final word. It means hope is real.

The Takeaway

Suffering doesn't cancel out God—it reveals our need for Him. While evil hurts and can leave us questioning, it also points to a deeper truth: we live in a broken world that was once good and is being redeemed. God doesn't ignore pain—He entered it through Jesus and promises one day to end it completely. Until then, we can trust that He is near, working, and using even our pain to shape us for His purpose.

Journaling Prompts

1. What's a time in your life when pain made you question God—or draw closer to Him?

2. How does knowing Jesus suffered too affect the way you see your own pain?

3. What do you think God might be shaping in you through a current struggle?

4. Are there any areas where you're tempted to give up hope? Talk to God about them.

5. Write a prayer asking God to give you strength, perspective, and peace in suffering.

Chapter 11

CAN YOU ACTUALLY KNOW GOD? LIKE, REALLY KNOW HIM?

"Knowing God without knowing our own wretchedness makes for pride. Knowing our own wretchedness without knowing God makes for despair. Knowing Jesus Christ strikes the balance."
— *Blaise Pascal*

"I'm not into religion. I want something real. If God's real, why does He feel so far away?"
— *Jacob, age 17*

"This is eternal life: that they know you, the only true God, and Jesus Christ, whom you have sent."
— *John 17:3*

There's a difference between *knowing about* someone and *knowing* them. You can follow someone on social media, know their favorite drink order and where they went on vacation last summer, and still not know their heart at all. It's the same with God. A lot of people believe He exists, even talk about Him from time to time, but never actually know Him.

But what if knowing God isn't just possible—it's the whole point of life?

When Jesus prayed in John 17:3, He didn't say, "Eternal life is believing the right facts about God" or "doing good stuff for God." He said, "Eternal life is *knowing* God." A relationship. Real connection. Not just Sunday school answers or verses memorized, but walking with the living God day by day. That's what your soul was created for.

In this chapter, we'll look at why it makes sense to believe that a personal God exists—and how you can actually know Him for yourself.

Wait, Is It Even Possible to Know God?

Let's start with the big question: Can you really know God, or is that just something Christians say to make themselves feel spiritual?

The Bible claims over and over that God *wants* to be known. Jeremiah 9:24 says, "Let the one who boasts boast about this: that they have the understanding to know me." God isn't hiding like a divine version of hide-and-seek. He's revealed Himself—through creation, through Scripture, and most clearly, through Jesus.

Think about it: if the universe had a beginning (and it did), and it's not eternal (which science supports), then whatever caused it must be timeless, powerful, and immaterial. Philosophers and scientists call this the First Cause. Christians call Him *God*. But He's not just a distant force—He's personal. The fact that we can love, reason, create, and desire truth suggests that the source of our being is personal too.

It would be strange to believe that we humans, who crave relationships and meaning, were made by a Creator who has no personality or desire to connect. From Genesis to Revelation, the God of the Bible is relational. He walks with Adam, talks with Moses, calls Abraham His friend, and through Jesus, calls us sons and daughters.

More Than Facts: A Relationship, Not a Religion

You've probably heard this before: Christianity is not a religion, it's a relationship. That's not just a cheesy phrase—it's a radical truth.

Religion says, "Do these things to reach God." Relationship says, "God came to you."

Religion says, "Check the boxes." Relationship says, "Walk with Me."

Religion leaves you exhausted, wondering if you've done enough. Relationship invites you to rest in love that isn't earned but given.

Jesus didn't die to start a new religion. He died to make it possible for you to be reconciled to God. That means no more guilt walling you off from Him. No more trying to impress Him. Just grace. Just presence. Just Him.

But like any relationship, knowing God requires time, trust, and openness. You can't know someone if you're never around them or if you always hide your heart. The same is true with God.

How Do You Get to Know God Personally?

Knowing God isn't about being super spiritual—it's about being real. It starts with a simple decision to believe that Jesus is who He said He is and to receive Him as Savior and Lord. That's the foundation.

But then it grows. You get to know God the way you get to know anyone: by spending time together. Through prayer, where you talk and listen. Through Scripture, where God's voice speaks to your heart. Through community, where other believers walk with you and help you see God more clearly.

And through life—every win, every heartbreak, every ordinary moment—God is speaking. The more you open your heart, the more you realize He's been there all along.

But What If I Don't Feel Close to God?

Good question. There will be seasons when God feels distant. Dry spells where you pray and it feels like nothing happens. You're not weird. You're not broken. You're human.

Even David, the "man after God's own heart," cried out, "Why, O Lord, do you hide your face from me?" (Psalm 88:14). Even Jesus on the cross cried, "My God, my God, why have you forsaken me?" (Matthew 27:46).

Feelings aren't the whole story. Faith is deeper than emotion. Sometimes God lets us feel the silence to build our trust. Sometimes He's working under the surface in ways we can't yet see. But He hasn't left. If you've trusted Jesus, God lives in you by His Spirit. That's not a metaphor. It's reality.

So when He feels far, don't fake it. Tell Him. Be honest. Then keep showing up. Keep seeking. Keep trusting. Often, the moments that feel empty become the soil for the deepest roots of faith.

If God Knows Me, Why Bother Knowing Him Back?

God knows you better than you know yourself. Psalm 139 says He knit you together in your mother's womb and knows your thoughts before you think them. So why bother trying to know Him back?

Because love isn't complete without relationship.

Imagine having a friend who knows everything about you but never talks to you. That would be weird. One-sided. Incomplete.

God doesn't want to be a distant observer in your life. He wants to be your Shepherd, your Father, your closest Friend. When you begin to know Him—really know Him—you discover who *you* really are. Your identity. Your purpose. Your joy. That's the invitation.

Jesus said in John 10:14, "I am the good shepherd; I know my sheep and my sheep know me." That's intimacy. That's connection. That's real.

The Takeaway

Yes, you really can know Him!

God isn't just a concept or a distant power. He is a person—a loving, holy, just, and merciful God who invites you into relationship. Through Jesus, the way has been made open. You don't have to wonder if God cares or if you matter. You do. And He wants you to know Him—not just facts or theology, but His heart, His presence, His love.

It takes time. It takes seeking. But it's worth everything. Because at the end of the day, the goal of your faith isn't to be religious. It's to know God.

Prayer

God, I want to know You—not just know *about* You, but to truly know You. To walk with You, talk with You, trust You. Sometimes You feel distant, and I don't always understand what You're doing. But I believe You're real, and I believe You want to be close. So here I am. I open my heart. Teach me who You are. Show me Your love. Help me seek You with all I've got. And when I mess up or feel lost, remind me that You haven't left. You are faithful. And You are enough. In Jesus' name, Amen.

Journaling Prompts

1. How would you describe your relationship with God right now—close, distant, confused, growing?

2. What are some things that get in the way of you feeling connected to God?

3. When have you felt most aware of God's presence in your life?

4. What are some specific ways you can grow in knowing God this week?

5. Write a letter to God telling Him what you really want in your relationship with Him.

Part Two: The Cross

Looking Closer—
Who Was Jesus, and Why Does It Matter?

Once you've looked at the evidence for *a* God, it's time to ask the bigger question: *Which God?*

Because believing in "something" out there isn't enough. The real challenge is figuring out who that "something" is—and whether we can know Him personally.

Enter Jesus.

In this part, we'll take a serious look at the most famous person in history. Not just the Sunday school version or the social media caricature. The real Jesus. We'll explore the historical evidence for His life, His teachings, and—most shockingly—His death and resurrection.

We'll ask things like:

- Was Jesus even real, or just a legend?
- Did He *actually* claim to be God?
- Why was He crucified, and did He rise from the dead—or is that just a made-up miracle story?

These aren't small questions. Because if Jesus really did rise, then Christianity isn't just another religion—it's a rescue mission. And it changes everything about who you are, what your life means, and where you're going.

Get ready to look past the surface and confront the most important question of your life: *What will you do with Jesus?*

Chapter 12

DID JESUS REALLY EXIST?

> "Even if Jesus didn't rise from the dead, he still would have been the most influential figure in human history."
> — *Malcolm Muggeridge*

> "I'm not even a Christian, but you can't deny Jesus changed the world. That's just fact."
> — *Teen on Reddit*

> "For we did not follow cleverly devised stories when we told you about the coming of our Lord Jesus Christ in power, but we were eyewitnesses of his majesty."
> — *2 Peter 1:16 (NIV)*

Have you ever wondered if Jesus was even real? Maybe you've seen TikToks or YouTube videos saying Jesus is just a copycat myth based on ancient gods like Horus or Mithras. Maybe you've heard people say, "There's no real evidence Jesus ever lived." When you hear that enough, it can start to mess with your head.

So let's stop and ask the question: Did Jesus of Nazareth—a man who walked around in sandals, taught with authority, and was crucified on a Roman cross—actually exist in history? Or is he just part of a religious fairytale passed down for generations?

Before we can wrestle with who Jesus is, we have to settle whether He was ever here in the first place. If Jesus never walked the dusty roads of first-century Galilee, then Christianity is just an elaborate legend waiting to be shelved beside Greek myths. If He did live, then His life—and the claims attached to it—demand thoughtful attention. Historians approach this question the same way detectives solve cold cases: by weighing documents, cross-examining witnesses, and looking for corroborating evidence. Let's follow their trail.

This chapter isn't just about proving Jesus existed. It's about showing how history, both Christian and non-Christian, points to a real man who changed everything—and how that reality invites us to know Him for ourselves.

What History Tells Us

Let's start with the facts. Almost all serious historians—Christian, atheist, Jewish, agnostic, and everything in between—agree that Jesus of Nazareth existed. That's not some church-made claim; it's a historical consensus.

Historians aren't time travelers, but they've got solid methods for figuring out what happened long ago. They don't just rely on feelings or guesses—they look for reliable documents and eyewitness accounts, and they use some helpful tools. For example, they check whether different sources agree with each other (that's called multiple attestation), whether a story includes embarrassing or unlikely details (because those are less likely to be made up), and whether even enemies admit something happened. Using these tools, historians examine Jesus the same way they study people like Julius Caesar or Alexander the Great.

Dr. Bart Ehrman, an agnostic New Testament scholar who often critiques Christian beliefs, said, "The reality is that every single expert in the field of early Christianity, of any persuasion, agrees that Jesus existed." That's not exactly a church-promo quote. Ehrman has no stake in convincing people to follow Jesus. And yet, even he says the idea that Jesus didn't exist is "not taken seriously by scholars."

Evidence from Non-Christian Sources

You might think the only people who wrote about Jesus were His followers. But that's not true. Several ancient historians who didn't believe in Him still wrote about Him.

Roman historian Tacitus wrote around AD 116 about how Emperor Nero blamed Christians for the fire in Rome. Tacitus noted that Christians got their name from "Christus," who "suffered the extreme penalty during the reign of Tiberius at the hands of one of our procurators, Pontius Pilatus."

That's not a believer talking. That's a Roman historian confirming that Jesus existed and was executed under Pilate—just like the Gospels say.

Then there's Josephus, a Jewish historian writing in the first century. He mentions Jesus in his writings, calling him "a wise man… a doer of wonderful works." Although parts of his writings may have been edited later by Christians, most scholars agree the core statement about Jesus is authentic.

Even Lucian of Samosata, a second-century Greek satirist who poked fun at Christians, confirmed Jesus was crucified and had followers who worshipped him.

Other Roman writers like Pliny the Younger and Suetonius also referred to early Christians and "Chrestus," which is probably a misspelling of Christ. Even the Jewish Talmud, which was very critical of Jesus, still admits that He was crucified. These aren't friendly sources, but they all agree on one key point: Jesus was a real person who lived and was executed.

Author	Date Written	What He Says
Tacitus (Roman senator)	c. A.D. 115	Mentions "Christus," executed under Pontius Pilate during Tiberius' reign, and notes the stubborn growth of the movement in Rome.
Josephus (Jewish historian)	c. A.D. 93	Refers twice to Jesus: once as "a wise man…crucified under Pilate," and again naming James "the brother of Jesus called Christ."
Pliny the Younger (Roman governor)	c. A.D. 112	Reports that Christians in Bithynia sing hymns "to Christ as to a god."
Suetonius (Roman biographer)	c. A.D. 120	Mentions disturbances in Rome instigated by someone called "Chrestus."
The Babylonian Talmud (Jewish rabbinic commentary)	2nd–5th centuries	Confirms that Jesus was "hanged on the eve of Passover," a Jewish idiom for crucifixion.

What the Christian Sources Tell Us

The Bible is obviously the main source of information about Jesus, but it's not just one book—it's a collection of 27 different writings from people who lived in the first century. The New Testament includes letters from Paul that were written only 20 to 30 years after Jesus' death. In one of them, 1 Corinthians 15, Paul shares a list of eyewitnesses who saw Jesus alive after His death. This list is believed to be based on a creed that dates to just a few years after the crucifixion. That's incredibly early by historical standards. Then we have the Gospels—Matthew, Mark, Luke, and John—which give us detailed stories of Jesus' life, teachings, and death. These accounts were written while many eyewitnesses were still alive, and even though they tell the same big story, they do so from different angles, which actually makes them more believable.

Does the Evidence Hold Up?

Let's test this like historians do. First, we have multiple sources saying the same thing—Roman historians, Jewish texts, Paul's letters, and the four Gospels. That's powerful. Second, there are things in the Gospel stories that are hard to explain if someone were making them up—like Jesus being rejected by His own family, betrayed by a close friend, and crucified like a criminal. If the early Christians wanted to make Jesus look like a superhero, they wouldn't have included those things. Third, even Jesus' enemies confirmed the basics. They didn't say He was fake—they just accused Him of magic or blasphemy, which shows they believed He existed.

Archaeology Agrees

While archaeology can't give us a photo of Jesus, it can show whether the places and people mentioned in the Bible were real. And so far, it does. For example, a stone discovered in Caesarea includes the name of Pontius Pilate, the very Roman governor who sentenced Jesus to die. Excavations have confirmed that Nazareth existed in Jesus' time and that synagogues in places like Capernaum really were there. All of this lines up with what the Gospels describe.

What Do Scholars Say?

Believe it or not, almost all serious historians—whether they're Christians, atheists, or somewhere in between—agree that Jesus was a real person who lived and was crucified. That includes skeptical scholars like Bart Ehrman, who doesn't believe Jesus was God, but strongly argues that Jesus definitely existed. The tiny number of people who claim Jesus was a myth are often not historians at all. Their arguments tend to fall apart under real academic scrutiny. Saying "Jesus never existed" today is kind of like saying "The earth is flat"—it just doesn't hold up.

What About Common Objections?

Some people say there aren't any official Roman records of Jesus' trial, so He must not have existed. But that's not a strong argument.

We don't have Roman records for most people from that time, even famous ones. Paper didn't last long, and most documents have been lost. Others claim the Jesus story borrowed from ancient myths, like dying and rising gods. But those so-called "parallels" usually came after Christianity started, or they're way too different to matter. No ancient myth has a real person crucified by Rome, buried in a specific tomb, and then claimed to be risen by hundreds of eyewitnesses. Jesus' story stands alone.

Why It Matters

It's one thing to believe Jesus existed, but why does it matter to you sitting in math class or scrolling your phone? Because if Jesus really lived—and especially if He rose from the dead—then what He said and did affects everything.

The existence of Jesus is the starting point. If He didn't exist, then Christianity falls apart. But if He did exist—and history says He did—then we have to wrestle with what kind of person He was. Was He just a wise teacher? A misunderstood prophet? Or was He exactly who He claimed to be: the Son of God who came to rescue us?

The reality of Jesus grounds your faith in something real. You're not following a legend or spiritual idea. You're following a person who lived, died, and rose again.

Still Skeptical?

It's okay to ask questions. God isn't afraid of your doubts. In fact, asking hard questions is part of growing a deeper, more resilient faith. If someone tells you that believing in Jesus is like believing in unicorns or fairytales, you now have tools to push back.

Jesus' existence isn't wishful thinking. It's rooted in history. And that history demands a response. You can't just shrug Jesus off as a myth once you realize how much evidence points to His real life. You either lean in and ask more—or walk away on purpose. But you can't stay neutral once you see the facts.

A Real Relationship With a Real Person

The most amazing part of this whole conversation? Jesus isn't just someone who *existed*. He's someone who *exists*—right now. Christianity isn't about memorizing facts or defending ancient history. It's about knowing a Person. A living Savior who knows you, loves you, and invites you into real relationship.

Because He lived in history, we can know Him in the present.

Because He walked this earth, we can walk with Him now.

Because He faced suffering and death, He understands ours.

And because He rose again, He offers hope that doesn't end.

The Takeaway

The question, "Did Jesus really exist?" has a clear answer: Yes. History—both inside and outside the Bible—confirms it. Jesus of Nazareth was not a myth, but a man who lived, taught, was crucified, and whose story has changed billions of lives. But that history isn't just a fact to memorize. It's a door to step through. If Jesus really lived, the next question is: Will you follow Him?

Prayer

> God, sometimes it's hard to tell what's real anymore. I hear so many voices saying different things. But if Jesus really lived—and I believe He did—then I want to know Him for who He truly is. Not just someone I hear about in church, but someone I can talk to, walk with, and trust. Help me understand more. Help me follow with a heart that's open, even when I doubt. Thank You for being a God who stepped into history so I could know You. In Jesus' name, Amen.

Journal Prompts

1. What's something new you learned about the historical evidence for Jesus?

2. Why do you think it's important that Jesus' life is confirmed by non-Christian sources?

3. How does knowing Jesus really lived affect how you see Him today?

4. What are some of your honest doubts about Jesus? Have you talked to God about them?

5. If Jesus was truly a real person who claimed to be God, what does that mean for your life right now?

Chapter 13

WHAT DID JESUS ACTUALLY LOOK LIKE? AND DOES IT EVEN MATTER?

"Jesus may have looked like an average guy in the street. But He turned the world upside down. That tells you something about what really matters."
— *Teen Bible Study Leader*

"We do not know what He looked like, but we know what He loved like."
— *Max Lucado*

"He had no beauty or majesty to attract us to him, nothing in his appearance that we should desire him."
— *Isaiah 53:2b (NIV)*

If someone says "Jesus," what image pops into your mind? Maybe a soft-spoken man with long, wavy hair, glowing skin, and a perfectly trimmed beard. Maybe He's wearing a white robe with a blue sash, standing in a peaceful meadow with sheep. For many people, the picture of Jesus they've grown up with looks more like a Hollywood actor than a first-century Middle Eastern man.

But have you ever stopped to ask: What did Jesus *actually* look like? Does the Bible give any description? Does history? And honestly—why do we even care?

This chapter explores those questions not just to satisfy curiosity but to help you connect with who Jesus really was—and still is. Because as we'll see, Jesus' physical appearance may surprise you, but it might also shift the way you see yourself, others, and God.

No Selfies, No Sketches

First things first: there are no verified drawings or paintings of Jesus from His lifetime. No one pulled out a sketchpad during the Sermon on the Mount. And the Gospels don't spend time describing what He looked like physically.

Why? Because His appearance wasn't the point.

The earliest Christians were more focused on *who* Jesus was and *what* He did than what He looked like. In fact, the only real physical description we get comes from the prophet Isaiah, written hundreds of years before Jesus was born. Isaiah 53:2 says He had "no beauty or majesty… nothing in His appearance that we should desire Him." In other words, Jesus didn't stand out physically. He looked ordinary.

What Did Jesus Actually Look Like? And Does It Even Matter?

A Brown-Skinned, Middle Eastern Man

Although we don't have exact details, we do know Jesus was a Jewish man born in the Middle East. He likely had olive or darker skin, dark hair, and brown eyes. He probably wore a simple tunic, sandals, and a head covering like other men of His time. His hands may have been rough from working as a carpenter.

In 2001, British scientists and Israeli archaeologists used forensic anthropology to reconstruct what a first-century Jewish man might have looked like. The result was a far cry from the blonde-haired, blue-eyed Jesus in many Western paintings. This Jesus had dark skin, short curly hair, and a strong build. Of course, this wasn't an exact image of Jesus—but it was likely closer than the versions many of us have seen.

Does that shake your picture of Jesus a little? It should—and that's not a bad thing.

Why We Want Jesus to Look Like Us

Part of the reason people have painted Jesus in so many different ways—Black Jesus, Asian Jesus, European Jesus—is because we want to feel connected to Him. That's not necessarily wrong. God came to earth in a human body so we *could* relate to Him. But there's also a danger when we try to make Jesus fit our image instead of reshaping *our* image around Him.

Jesus didn't come for one ethnicity or culture. He came for *all*. And maybe one of the most beautiful truths of Christianity is that people of every background, race, and language can see themselves welcomed in the family of God—not because Jesus looked like them, but because He *loved* them.

Beyond the Surface

Jesus was the kind of person you might have passed on the street without noticing. But those who *did* notice—who stopped to listen, to follow—found themselves changed forever.

We live in a world that's obsessed with appearances. Social media constantly bombards us with messages that say your worth is tied to how you look. But Jesus flipped that upside down. He had no flashy looks, no special glow, yet people left everything to follow Him. Why? Because He carried a love, a truth, and a presence that went far deeper than appearances.

Seeing Jesus in Others

When we think about what Jesus really looked like, we're also invited to look differently at the people around us. Jesus said in Matthew 25 that when we serve the hungry, the poor, the sick, the lonely—we're serving *Him*. That means the face of Jesus is reflected in others, especially in the overlooked.

When you're tempted to judge someone based on how they look—or when you feel less-than because of how *you* look—remember this: Jesus sees beyond appearances. And so should we.

So… Does It Even Matter?

Yes and no. No, because Jesus' physical appearance doesn't change His power, truth, or love. But yes, because understanding who Jesus really was in history grounds your faith in reality. And yes, because realizing Jesus probably looked different than your mental picture reminds you that God's love isn't tied to outward appearance. It reaches into every tribe, tongue, and skin tone.

More than anything, what matters is what's happening on the inside. What kind of character did Jesus have? What kind of compassion did He show? What kind of hope did He give? Those are the traits we're called to reflect—not His face, but His heart.

Summary: What Really Matters

We don't know exactly what Jesus looked like, but we know this: He was real, human, ordinary in appearance, and extraordinary in every other way. He didn't come to impress with outward beauty but to rescue us with divine love. And that love is still calling you today—not to be beautiful by the world's standards, but to be transformed by His grace.

A Prayer to See What Really Matters

Jesus, I admit I've sometimes focused more on appearances—mine, others', even Yours—than on what really matters. Thank You for coming into the world in a way that was humble and human. Help me see You more clearly, not through the lens of culture, but through the truth of who You are. Help me reflect Your heart more than trying to copy a certain look. Change how I see others. And change how I see myself. Teach me to look beyond the surface and love like You do. Amen.

What Did Jesus Actually Look Like? And Does It Even Matter?

Journal Prompts

1. What image of Jesus did you grow up with? How has that shaped the way you think about Him?

2. Does it make a difference to you knowing Jesus likely had dark skin and Middle Eastern features? Why or why not?

3. Have you ever felt judged or treated differently based on your appearance? How might Jesus understand that?

4. What are some ways you can reflect Jesus' character more than just focusing on your appearance?

5. Who around you might be overlooked by others—but seen and loved by Jesus?

Chapter 14

DID JESUS CLAIM TO BE GOD?

> "A man who was merely a man and said the sort of things Jesus said would not be a great moral teacher. He would either be a lunatic—or he would be the Devil of Hell. You must make your choice."
> — *C.S. Lewis*

> "If Jesus never claimed to be God, then why did they kill Him for blasphemy?"
> — *Teen in a small group Bible study*

> "Very truly I tell you, before Abraham was born, I am!"
> — *John 8:58 (NIV)*

Have you ever had a moment when someone said something so bold, so outrageous, that the room went silent? Like when someone stands up in the cafeteria and sings out loud, or when a friend says something that makes everyone stop and stare. That's what Jesus did—but on a whole different level.

People loved Jesus for His teachings, His compassion, His miracles—but they also hated Him. Not just because He was different, but because He claimed something that no other religious leader has ever dared to say: that He was God in the flesh.

That's a massive claim. So the question is, did He actually say it? Or did people just say it about Him later on?

Let's dive into the Gospels and history to find out if Jesus claimed to be God—and what that means for you today.

The Subtle Power of Jewish Context

If you're looking for a place where Jesus stood on a mountain and yelled, "Hey everyone, I'm God!" you won't find it. But that doesn't mean He didn't claim it.

Jesus lived in a deeply Jewish culture where declaring yourself as God directly could get you killed immediately—and it did. But He spoke in ways that His Jewish audience totally understood as divine claims. The religious leaders knew exactly what He meant, and they were furious.

For example, in John 10:30, Jesus says, "I and the Father are one." The very next verse says, "Again his Jewish opponents picked up stones to stone him." Why? Because in their eyes, that was blasphemy—a man claiming to be God.

Then there's John 8:58. Jesus tells the crowd, "Before Abraham was born, I am." That might not sound crazy to us, but to Jews, this was sacred. "I AM" was the name God gave Moses at the burning bush (Exodus 3:14). So when Jesus said this, He was claiming the eternal identity of God Himself. That's why people picked up stones to kill Him right there. They understood.

Jesus Forgave Sins (Like Only God Can)

Another thing Jesus did that made religious leaders furious? He forgave sins. In Mark 2, a paralyzed man is brought to Jesus, and Jesus says, "Son, your sins are forgiven." People around Him freak out: "Who can forgive sins but God alone?"

Exactly.

Only God has the authority to erase sin, because all sin is ultimately against Him. By forgiving sins, Jesus wasn't just acting kindly—He was making a bold, divine statement.

Jesus Accepted Worship

Throughout the Gospels, Jesus is worshipped—and not just once. In Matthew 14:33, after Jesus walks on water and calms the storm, His disciples worship Him, saying, "Truly you are the Son of God."

He doesn't stop them. He doesn't say, "Whoa, I'm just a prophet." He receives their worship.

When the resurrected Jesus appears to Thomas in John 20, Thomas falls and says, "My Lord and my God!" Jesus doesn't correct him. He confirms it.

Contrast this with angels or apostles in Scripture who are always quick to say, "Don't worship me!" when people try. Jesus never does.

The Trial That Sealed It

One of the clearest moments comes during Jesus' trial. In Mark 14:61–62, the high priest asks Jesus directly: "Are you the Messiah, the Son of the Blessed One?"

Jesus answers, "I am... And you will see the Son of Man sitting at the right hand of the Mighty One and coming on the clouds of heaven."

That reference to "Son of Man" and "coming on the clouds" is straight from Daniel 7—a vision of divine authority. The priest tore his clothes and called it blasphemy. He knew Jesus wasn't just claiming to be a good teacher. He was claiming to be the eternal King.

That claim cost Jesus His life.

Could Jesus Be Lying—or Just Wrong?

Some people try to sidestep this issue by saying Jesus never meant to be taken literally. Maybe He was just a spiritual guru, misunderstood by His followers.

But if that's true, why was He executed? Why did so many people—Jews and Romans alike—think He was dangerous enough to kill?

Jesus' words and actions don't leave room for Him to be "just a good guy." C.S. Lewis famously said Jesus is either a liar, a lunatic, or the Lord. Those are the only real options. You can't say He was just nice and wise. He claimed too much.

Why It Changes Everything

If Jesus claimed to be God—and all signs say He did—then you can't just scroll past Him. You have to decide: Do you believe Him?

Because if Jesus is God, then knowing Him is the most important thing you'll ever do. And if He's not, then Christianity collapses.

But here's the beauty: The God Jesus claimed to be isn't distant or cold. He's the God who came near. Who wept. Who healed. Who carried a cross.

He claimed to be God not to dominate us—but to rescue us.

He didn't just tell people who He was; He showed them.

And He still does.

The Takeaway

Jesus really did claim to be God. He never whispered about His identity. He said things and did things only God could do—and everyone around Him knew it. He forgave sins, accepted worship, fulfilled prophecy, and used divine names. His trial and execution were based on His claim to be God. So if you've ever wondered whether He really made that claim, the answer is yes.

Now the question becomes: What will you do with that truth?

Prayer

> Jesus, I don't want to build my life on a fake version of You. I want to know who You really are. If You truly claimed to be God—and I believe You did—then I want to follow You with my whole heart. Help me not to brush past Your words, but to take them seriously. Thank You for not just saying You're God, but for showing us through love, sacrifice, and grace. Draw me closer to You. Help me believe, even in my doubts. Amen.

Journal Prompts

1. What's one thing in this chapter that surprised or challenged you?

2. Why do you think Jesus used indirect ways to claim He was God instead of shouting it outright?

3. How does it affect your view of Jesus to know He accepted worship and forgave sins?

4. If Jesus really is God, what part of your life needs to come under His authority?

5. Write out your honest thoughts: Do you believe Jesus is who He said He is? Why or why not?

Chapter 15

DID JESUS REALLY DIE ON THE CROSS?

> "Truth is like the sun. You can shut it out for a time, but it ain't goin' away."
> —*Elvis Presley*

> "The empty tomb is proof that the Cross was not the end."
> —*Anonymous*

> "But he was pierced for our transgressions, he was crushed for our iniquities; the punishment that brought us peace was on him, and by his wounds we are healed."
> —*Isaiah 53:5*

There's no denying it: the cross is the most recognized symbol of Christianity. We wear it as jewelry, hang it on our walls, and see it standing tall on church steeples. But have you ever stopped to ask, "Did Jesus *really* die on a cross?" Was His death a historical event, or just a religious story? Did He actually suffer crucifixion, or is it just part of a spiritual myth told by the early church to inspire followers?

These questions are important—because the entire message of Christianity rests on the reality of Jesus' death. If Jesus didn't die, then there's no real sacrifice, no resurrection, and ultimately, no salvation. So let's take a close look at the evidence: historical, medical, and logical. You might be surprised just how solid it really is.

Non-Christian Historical Records

We don't just believe Jesus died on a cross because the Bible says so—though the Bible *does* give detailed, eyewitness accounts (see Matthew 27, Mark 15, Luke 23, and John 19). But even outside of Scripture, ancient historians confirm Jesus' death.

Tacitus, a Roman historian writing around A.D. 116, refers to Jesus' execution:

> "Christus, from whom the name [Christian] had its origin, suffered the extreme penalty during the reign of Tiberius at the hands of...Pontius Pilate." *(Annals 15.44)*

"The extreme penalty" was a Roman term for crucifixion.

Josephus, a Jewish historian writing around A.D. 93, mentions that Jesus was "condemned to the cross by Pilate" (Antiquities 18.3.3). Though some portions of his writings were later altered by Christians, most scholars agree that Josephus did refer to Jesus' crucifixion.

Lucian of Samosata, a Greek satirist from the second century, mocked Christians for worshiping someone who was crucified. His ridicule ironically confirms the event:

> "...the man who was crucified in Palestine because he introduced this new cult into the world."

In short, ancient secular historians—who had no reason to promote Christianity—acknowledged that Jesus was crucified. His death wasn't a legend invented centuries later; it was known, recorded, and remembered.

Roman Crucifixion: Brutal and Undeniably Fatal

Some skeptics claim that Jesus didn't actually die—that He just passed out and later recovered in the tomb. But this idea doesn't line up with what we know about Roman crucifixion.

The Romans were experts in execution. Crucifixion was designed to be slow, public, and excruciating. Victims were beaten, stripped, nailed to wooden beams, and left to hang for hours or days. The goal wasn't just death—it was humiliation and maximum suffering.

Jesus was:

- Scourged with a Roman whip (John 19:1), a process that tore flesh from the back and often exposed muscle and bone.

- Forced to carry His own cross until He collapsed from exhaustion (Mark 15:21).

- Nailed through the wrists and feet—a method that caused intense nerve pain and made breathing difficult.

- Suspended in a way that required pushing up on pierced feet to inhale, which led to suffocation as the body weakened.

John 19:34 tells us that after Jesus' death, a Roman soldier pierced His side with a spear, and "immediately blood and water came out"—which many believe was a sign of a ruptured heart or fluid-filled lungs. Medical professionals today recognize this as evidence of death.

Crucifixion was so effective that no Roman soldier could allow a victim to survive. If someone *did* survive execution, the soldier responsible could face death himself. So when Pilate was surprised Jesus died "so soon" (Mark 15:44), he double-checked with the centurion. Only after confirming Jesus was dead did he allow the body to be taken down.

The Burial and the Empty Tomb

Jesus' dead body was not tossed in a ditch or left unclaimed. Instead, He was buried in a tomb owned by a well-known man, Joseph of Arimathea, a member of the Jewish council (Luke 23:50–

53). This means Jesus' burial was public and verifiable. His tomb location was known.

And yet, three days later, His followers began boldly proclaiming that He had risen from the dead—and His tomb was empty.

If Jesus had simply fainted or been taken down alive, He wouldn't have had the strength to roll away a massive stone, sneak past armed Roman guards, and convince people He was the victorious Son of God. The disciples were convinced of the resurrection, not because of blind faith, but because they had seen the Risen Christ.

But that resurrection depends on the crucifixion actually happening—and it did.

Why Would They Make It Up?

Some say the story of Jesus' death was invented. But if it were a lie, it's a terrible one—for a few reasons:

- **Crucifixion was shameful.** In Jewish law, anyone "hung on a tree is cursed by God" (Deuteronomy 21:23). Why would early Christians invent a death that made their leader seem cursed?

- **The disciples were terrified at first**, hiding in fear. Something dramatic had to happen to turn them into bold preachers willing to die for their message (Acts 5:29–32).

They didn't make up the cross—they proclaimed it because they saw its power.

- **All of Jesus' closest followers were willing to suffer and die,** not for a lie they invented, but for a truth they believed down to their bones. Liars make poor martyrs.

Why Some People Doubt

So why do people still question whether Jesus really died? For some, it's hard to believe in miracles, like the Resurrection. If Jesus didn't die, then maybe the Resurrection was just a myth or a misunderstanding. Others may feel threatened by what His death means—because if He really did die for our sins, then we have to wrestle with the reality of our own sin, our need for grace, and our response to His sacrifice.

Sometimes, it's just easier to doubt than to believe.

But doubting isn't wrong. It can actually lead to a deeper faith when we bring our questions to God and seek truth. God isn't afraid of your doubts. In fact, He welcomes them. He wants you to search, learn, ask, and discover that His truth holds up.

The Evidence Speaks

Historians, even those who don't believe Jesus was the Son of God, agree that He died by crucifixion. Sources outside the Bible—like the Roman historian Tacitus and the Jewish historian Josephus—confirm that Jesus was executed under Pontius Pilate. These aren't Christian sources; they're historical records from people who had no reason to promote Christianity. That makes their testimony even more powerful.

The disciples, who had been terrified and hiding after Jesus' arrest, suddenly became bold proclaimers of His resurrection. They didn't act like people who were trying to protect a hoax. They believed with their whole hearts that Jesus had died and rose again—and they were willing to die for that belief. People don't usually die for something they know is a lie.

Jesus' death wasn't an accident or a tragic end to a good life. It was God's plan to deal with the sin that separates us from Him. That plan only works if Jesus really died. The cross is not just a symbol of suffering; it's a symbol of love, of sacrifice, and of the greatest rescue mission in history.

What This Means for You

Jesus' death wasn't an accident, a tragedy, or a myth—it was a sacrifice. Isaiah 53:5 says:

> "He was pierced for our transgressions,
> He was crushed for our iniquities;
> the punishment that brought us peace was on Him,
> and by His wounds we are healed."

The cross wasn't just an execution—it was an exchange. Jesus took the penalty we deserved so that we could be forgiven, free, and made right with God.

So what does this mean for your life? If Jesus really died on the cross, then it means your sin is not too big for God. It means you are loved so deeply that God Himself was willing to take your place. It means you don't have to carry shame, fear, or regret alone.

It also means that Jesus understands suffering. He's not distant from your pain. He's been through betrayal, agony, and abandonment. He gets it. And He meets you there—with love, not condemnation.

When you understand that Jesus really died for you, it changes how you see everything. Suddenly, faith isn't just about rules or religion. It's about a relationship with the One who gave everything so you could be free. The cross becomes personal. And from that place of understanding, you can begin to live in the light of His love, forgiveness, and grace.

The Takeaway

So, did Jesus really die on a cross?

Yes. Historically, medically, and logically—it's one of the most well-attested facts of the ancient world. But even more than that, the cross is a doorway. It's where God's love and justice met, and where your life can be forever changed.

Jesus didn't just die on a cross—**He died for you.**

Prayer

> Jesus, Thank You for the cross. Thank You for facing the worst kind of suffering so I wouldn't have to live forever in separation from You. Help me to believe, even when I have doubts. Give me eyes to see the truth, a heart open to Your love, and the courage to trust You. Remind me daily that Your death wasn't the end—it was the beginning of life, hope, and victory. Teach me to live in the freedom You won for me. I love You. Amen.

Journaling Prompts

1. What questions do I still have about Jesus' death? Who can I talk to about them?

2. How does knowing Jesus truly died for me change how I see my worth and identity?

3. When have I experienced doubt in my faith, and how did I deal with it?

4. What does the cross personally mean to me today?

5. How can I share the message of Jesus' death and resurrection with someone who might be struggling to believe it?

Chapter 16

DID JESUS REALLY RISE FROM THE DEAD? THE EVIDENCE YOU CAN'T IGNORE!

"Even if you're on the right track, you'll get run over if you just sit there."
—*Will Rogers*

"The resurrection gives my life meaning and direction and the opportunity to start over no matter what my circumstances."
—*Robert Flatt*

"He is not here; he has risen, just as he said. Come and see the place where he lay."
—*Matthew 28:6*

If someone told you their friend came back from the dead, you'd probably raise an eyebrow—maybe both. Let's be honest, it sounds wild. And that's exactly why the resurrection of Jesus is the most important claim in all of Christianity. If Jesus didn't rise from the dead, then Christianity is based on a lie. But if

He did rise, then everything changes—because death isn't the end anymore.

If you're a Christian—or even just curious about Christianity—there's no bigger question than this one: *Did Jesus really rise from the dead?* The entire Christian faith stands or falls on the truth of the resurrection. The Apostle Paul said it straight up in 1 Corinthians 15:17: *"If Christ has not been raised, your faith is futile; you are still in your sins."* In other words, if the resurrection didn't happen, Christianity is just a religious fairy tale.

But if Jesus *did* rise from the dead? That changes everything.

In this chapter, we're going to explore the resurrection of Jesus from historical, logical, and biblical angles. This isn't about blind faith—it's about *reasonable faith*. We're going to examine the evidence with open eyes, so you can decide for yourself what to believe.

1. What Is the Claim?

Let's clarify what Christians actually believe. The claim isn't that Jesus' teachings *lived on* in people's hearts, or that His disciples *felt inspired* by Him after His death. The claim is that Jesus of Nazareth—who was crucified under the Roman governor Pontius Pilate—*physically came back to life*, left behind an empty tomb, and appeared to hundreds of people over a period of 40 days before ascending into heaven.

That's a bold claim. But it's not the kind of claim you can ignore. Because if it's true, Jesus is more than just a good teacher—He's the Son of God, and we need to take everything He said seriously.

2. Is There Good Evidence for the Resurrection?

Yes. While we can't hop in a time machine to watch it happen, we *can* examine the historical evidence. Here are four key facts that most scholars—Christian and non-Christian—agree upon:

Fact #1: Jesus Died by Crucifixion

This might seem obvious, but it's important. Jesus' death by Roman crucifixion is one of the most well-attested facts of the ancient world. Roman historian Tacitus, Jewish historian Josephus, and even the Babylonian Talmud all confirm that Jesus was executed by crucifixion.

Roman executioners were professionals—they didn't make mistakes. Jesus was beaten, scourged, nailed to a cross, and pierced through with a spear. He didn't swoon. He died.

Fact #2: The Tomb Was Found Empty

The Gospels all report that Jesus' tomb was found empty on the third day. This claim is so early and widespread that even critics can't dismiss it easily. If Jesus' body had still been in the tomb, the Roman or Jewish authorities could have crushed the Christian movement by producing the corpse. But they didn't—because they couldn't.

Even the earliest critics of Christianity didn't deny the empty tomb. Instead, they claimed the disciples stole the body (Matthew 28:11–15). That argument actually *confirms* the tomb was empty—they just didn't agree on how.

When Jesus was buried, the tomb was sealed and guarded by Roman soldiers. These weren't lazy, careless guys. If they failed in their duty, their own lives could be at risk. Still, on Sunday morning, the tomb was empty.

The Jewish leaders and Roman authorities had every reason to prove that Jesus stayed dead. If they could have shown His body, Christianity would have died right there. But they couldn't—because the body was gone.

Some skeptics have claimed the disciples stole the body. But let's be real: terrified fishermen outsmarting Roman guards and then preaching a lie until they were executed for it? That's not likely. Others say maybe they went to the wrong tomb. But the women, the guards, the authorities—they all knew where Jesus was buried. The tomb was empty. And nobody could explain it away.

Fact #3: Jesus' Followers Believed They Saw Him Alive

After Jesus' death, His followers claimed they saw Him alive again. These weren't hallucinations or dreams. They said they touched

Him, ate with Him, and talked with Him. These weren't isolated events either—Jesus appeared to individuals, small groups, and even 500 people at once (1 Corinthians 15:3–8).

The Apostle Paul wrote in 1 Corinthians 15 that Jesus appeared to Peter, then the other disciples, and then to more than 500 people at once. He even said, "most of whom are still living," like, "Go ask them yourselves!" That's a bold claim to make if it's not true.

These weren't hallucinations or dreams. Hallucinations don't happen in groups, and they don't eat fish or let you touch them like Jesus did after His resurrection (see Luke 24:36–43, John 20:27). He wasn't a ghost. He was alive. Physical. Risen.

And the testimonies didn't just come from people who already believed in Him. James, Jesus' brother, didn't believe Jesus was the Son of God during His ministry. Let's be honest—how hard would it be to believe your own sibling is God? But after the resurrection, James became a leader in the early church and gave his life for the Gospel. That doesn't happen unless something life-altering takes place.

Some might say they were just making it up. But why would they lie? These same people were beaten, imprisoned, and killed for proclaiming the resurrection. People might die for something they *think* is true, but nobody dies for something they *know* is a lie.

Fact #4: The Church Exploded Out of Nowhere

One of the most powerful pieces of evidence that Jesus rose from the dead is how His followers responded. These were not gullible people waiting around for a miracle. They were heartbroken, scared, and scattered. When Jesus died, their hope died too. In their minds, it was over.

Then everything changed. These same disciples, who had gone into hiding, came out boldly claiming they had seen Jesus alive. Not just one of them—all of them. They didn't just say it quietly; they were so sure of it that they were willing to die for that belief. People don't willingly die for something they know is a lie. Something happened that turned their fear into unshakable faith.

Think about it: if the resurrection was a made-up story, how could it convince so many people, so fast, in such dangerous circumstances? The world flipped because something real had happened.

After Jesus' death, His scared and scattered followers suddenly became bold preachers of His resurrection. Within weeks, thousands in Jerusalem—the very city where He was crucified—became believers. That's not something that happens without something dramatic.

Jewish people weren't expecting a crucified Messiah. They had no concept of one person rising from the dead before the end of the world. The best explanation for their radical change is that something powerful actually happened—something like the resurrection.

If Jesus stayed dead, Christianity would have ended in the first century. The Messiah was supposed to conquer, not be crucified. That kind of ending would have crushed any normal movement. But instead of falling apart, it exploded. Not because of wishful thinking, but because something real happened. People had seen Jesus alive.

The early church grew rapidly—against all odds and in the face of violent persecution. No military, no money, no power. Just a message: Jesus is alive. That message turned the Roman Empire upside down.

Even today, millions of lives continue to be changed by this truth. That kind of transformation doesn't come from a legend. It comes from a risen Lord.

3. Are There Other Explanations?

Some people try to explain away the resurrection without saying it really happened. Let's look at a few of those theories—and why they don't hold up.

Theory 1: The Disciples Stole the Body

This was the earliest alternative explanation (see Matthew 28:13). But this theory falls apart quickly:

- The tomb was guarded by Roman soldiers. These weren't guys you could just sneak past.
- The disciples were terrified and hiding. Why would they suddenly become brave enough to steal a body and then die for a lie?
- No one dies for something they *know* they made up.

Theory 2: Jesus Didn't Really Die

Some say Jesus just fainted and later woke up in the tomb. But this doesn't make sense:

- Roman executioners knew how to kill people—they didn't let crucified criminals walk away alive.
- Even if Jesus had somehow survived, He would've been a broken, bleeding mess—not someone who could convince His followers He had conquered death.

Theory 3: The Disciples Hallucinated

Maybe the disciples were so sad and stressed that they just *imagined* Jesus came back. But hallucinations don't work that way:

- Hallucinations are individual, not group experiences. You don't get 500 people having the same vision at the same time.
- Hallucinations don't eat fish, cook breakfast, or walk with you for miles.

What Does This Mean for You?

If Jesus really rose from the dead, it means everything He said is true. It means your sin has been paid for. It means your future is not chained to your past. It means death doesn't get the final word.

You don't have to live afraid. You don't have to carry shame. You can walk in the power of a God who beat the grave. Jesus didn't rise to impress anyone. He rose to rescue everyone.

So when life feels heavy, when you're drowning in doubt, when everything seems broken—remember, the tomb is empty. Jesus is alive, and because He lives, you can have hope, no matter what.

The Takeaway

The resurrection of Jesus isn't just a historical fact to study—it's a life-changing reality to believe. It's backed by evidence, confirmed by eyewitnesses, and proven by transformed lives. Jesus really did rise from the dead. And that means there is hope for you, today and forever. The resurrection invites you into a story of freedom, grace, and victory over everything that tries to keep you down.

Prayer

> Jesus, Thank You for the cross, and thank You for the empty tomb. I believe that You really rose from the dead, and that because of that, I can have life that doesn't end. Help me to trust in You, especially when I have questions or doubts. Strengthen my faith, and help me live like someone who follows the risen King. Fill me with joy, courage, and purpose. I want to walk in the truth of Your resurrection every day. Amen.

Journaling Prompts

1. What doubts or questions do I have about the resurrection, and how can I explore them honestly?

2. How does knowing Jesus is alive change the way I face fear, guilt, or anxiety?

3. What part of the resurrection story speaks to me the most right now?

4. Who in my life needs to hear about the hope of the resurrection, and how can I share it?

5. How can I live each day with the confidence that Jesus is alive and walking with me?

Chapter 17

WHY WAS JESUS CRUCIFIED? IT'S MORE THAN YOU THINK!

> "The measure of love is to love without measure."
> —*Saint Augustine*

> "Real love is sacrificial."
> —*Sadie Robertson Huff*

> "Christ redeemed us from the curse of the law by becoming a curse for us—for it is written: 'Cursed is everyone who is hung on a pole.'"
> —*Galatians 3:13*

It's one of the most important questions anyone could ever ask: Why was Jesus crucified? If you've ever seen a cross hanging around someone's neck or displayed in a church, you've seen a symbol of the most famous death in all of history. But this was no ordinary execution. Jesus, the Son of God—perfect, innocent, and full of love—was put to death like a criminal. Why?

The answer takes us deep into the heart of the Christian faith. To truly understand why Jesus was crucified, we have to explore not only the events that led up to His death, but the bigger story that stretches from the beginning of time into eternity.

The Historical Reason: Rejected by the World

Jesus was crucified under the Roman government, specifically by order of the Roman governor Pontius Pilate. But the story begins long before that.

Jesus came preaching a message that challenged the religious leaders of His time. He spoke with authority, called out hypocrisy, healed the sick, raised the dead, and claimed to be the Son of God. Many ordinary people loved Him—but the powerful religious elites saw Him as a threat. The crowds that once followed Him turned against Him when He refused to be the kind of political savior they wanted. Betrayed by one of His closest friends, falsely accused, and unfairly tried, Jesus was sentenced to death.

The Roman method of execution—crucifixion—was brutal and shameful. It was designed to humiliate and torture the victim publicly. Jesus was mocked, beaten, whipped, and nailed to a cross where He hung for hours until He died.

From a historical viewpoint, Jesus was crucified because He upset the status quo. But that's only part of the picture. The bigger reason is far more meaningful.

The Theological Reason: The Problem of Sin

Here's the deeper truth: Jesus was crucified to deal with the problem of sin.

The Bible says that all human beings have sinned (Romans 3:23). That means we've all turned away from God in some way—whether through pride, lying, selfishness, anger, lust, or rebellion. Sin separates us from God, who is perfectly holy and just. And because God is just, He cannot ignore sin. It must be dealt with. The punishment for sin is death—both physical death and eternal separation from God (Romans 6:23).

But here's where God's incredible love enters the story.

God didn't want to leave us in our brokenness. So He sent His own Son—Jesus Christ—into the world. Jesus lived a perfect, sinless life. He obeyed God fully and never did anything wrong. And yet, Jesus willingly went to the cross, taking the punishment for our sin upon Himself.

Isaiah 53:5 says it like this:

> "But He was pierced for our transgressions, He was crushed for our iniquities; the punishment that brought us peace was on Him, and by His wounds we are healed."

Jesus wasn't just dying a martyr's death or making a political statement. He was sacrificing Himself in our place. This is what Christians call *substitutionary atonement*—Jesus took the punishment we deserved so we could be forgiven and made right with God.

The Personal Reason: Love for You

One of the most powerful truths in Scripture is this:

"God demonstrates His own love for us in this: While we were still sinners, Christ died for us" (Romans 5:8).

Jesus didn't die just to make a point—He died for **you**. He died to save you, to rescue you from the grip of sin, to give you a new life, and to restore your relationship with God.

Think about it: the perfect Son of God hung on a rough wooden cross, not because He had done anything wrong, but because He loved you so much that He couldn't bear to see you separated from the Father forever. Every nail driven into His body was not just an act of cruelty from man—it was also an act of love from heaven. Jesus chose the cross so you could choose eternal life.

The Eternal Reason: God's Victory Through Sacrifice

Jesus' crucifixion wasn't the end of the story. Three days later, He rose from the dead, conquering sin, death, and the grave. His resurrection proved that His sacrifice was accepted by God, and it opened the way for anyone—anyone—to be saved.

The cross is not a defeat. It is the greatest victory in history. It is where justice and mercy meet. At the cross, God punished sin without punishing the sinner. Instead, He sacrificed His own Son so that we might be free.

Because of the cross, forgiveness is possible. Because of the cross, you can be made new. Because of the cross, there is hope for your future.

So… Why Was Jesus Crucified?

Jesus was crucified to pay the price for your sins and mine.
He was crucified because God loves us too much to leave us lost.
He was crucified to take our place, bear our punishment, and bring us peace.
He was crucified so that we could be forgiven, healed, and restored.
He was crucified to rescue you—because He loves you more than you could ever imagine.

Let's get something straight: Jesus wasn't crucified because He was weak. He wasn't a victim of circumstance. He didn't get caught in the wrong place at the wrong time. Jesus was crucified on purpose—and for a purpose. A lot of people think the cross was just the sad end to a good life. But it was actually the greatest act of love the world has ever seen. It was brutal. It was bloody. And it was the only way to deal with something we all have: sin.

You might ask, "Why did it have to be so violent? Couldn't God just forgive us?" That's a real question. And the answer has to do with the seriousness of sin and the holiness of God. God is love, but He's also just. He doesn't ignore brokenness or evil. He confronts it—and then offers to fix it, no matter the cost to Himself. The crucifixion wasn't a mistake. It was a mission.

Who Really Put Jesus on the Cross?

Was it the Romans? The Jewish leaders? Was it Judas for betraying Him? Peter for denying Him? The crowd for shouting "Crucify Him!"? The answer is yes—to all of that. But it goes deeper. Jesus said in John 10:18, "No one takes it from me, but I lay it down of my own accord." He willingly gave His life. No one forced Him.

And if we're honest, we played a part too. Our sin—the lies, pride, jealousy, selfishness, and rebellion—is what made the cross necessary. It wasn't just a historical event; it was a spiritual rescue. Jesus went to the cross knowing your name, your struggles, your future. He went because He loves you that much.

This wasn't a backup plan. This was the plan all along. All of Scripture points to this moment, from the sacrifices of the Old Testament to the promises of the prophets. The cross is where God's justice and mercy collided—and it changed everything.

What the Cross Actually Did

When Jesus was crucified, He wasn't just dying a painful death. He was carrying the weight of the world's sin—including yours and mine. Paul says in 2 Corinthians 5:21, "God made him who had no sin to be sin for us, so that in him we might become the righteousness of God." That means Jesus took our place. The punishment we deserved? He bore it. The judgment we should have faced? He faced it instead.

The cross didn't just remove guilt—it broke the power of sin. Before Jesus, sin was a wall between us and God. After Jesus, that wall was torn down. The curtain in the temple, which separated people from God's presence, was ripped in two when He died (Matthew 27:51). That wasn't just a cool special effect. It was a spiritual earthquake. Jesus made a way for us to come close to God, not because we're good enough, but because He was.

The cross also defeated shame. Some of us live in fear that we'll never be enough. That we're too broken, too messed up. But Jesus' crucifixion says otherwise. He didn't die for the cleaned-up version of you. He died for the real, raw, struggling you. That's grace.

More Than Just Forgiveness

It would've been incredible enough if Jesus had just forgiven our sins. But He went further. He made us family. Through His death, we're not just saved—we're adopted. We're invited into a new life, a new identity, and a new relationship with God.

That means you're not defined by what you've done. You're defined by what Jesus has done for you. You don't have to earn His love. You live in response to it. The cross is proof that you matter, that your story is not over, and that God's love reaches further than your worst mistake.

It also means we don't just get to sit in the comfort of forgiveness—we're called to follow in Jesus' footsteps. The cross invites us into a life of sacrificial love, radical grace, and bold obedience. That doesn't mean it'll be easy, but it will be worth it.

A Love Story Written in Blood

There's no love like the love of Jesus. The crucifixion shows us a Savior who didn't just talk about love—He demonstrated it with every drop of blood. He could've walked away. He could've called down angels. He could've stayed silent. But He didn't.

He chose the cross. For you.

He chose it knowing the pain, the betrayal, the mockery. He chose it knowing that some people would still reject Him. He chose it not because we were lovable, but because He is love.

That kind of love changes people. It brings dead hearts to life. It breaks chains. It makes sinners into sons and daughters. And it gives us a new reason to live.

The Takeaway

Jesus was crucified not because He had to be, but because He chose to be. It was more than a punishment—it was a promise. A promise that sin doesn't win. That shame doesn't stick. That death isn't the end. The cross was where justice was served and mercy was offered. It was God saying, "I'll take the blame so you can come home."

And now, because of the cross, you're free to live fully, love deeply, and follow boldly.

A Prayer for Salvation

If you've never received what Jesus did for you on the cross—if you've never accepted His gift of forgiveness—now is the time. You don't need to clean up your life first. You just need to come to Him honestly, believing He died and rose again for you.

You can pray something like this:

> **Dear Jesus,**
> I believe You are the Son of God. I believe You died on the cross for my sins and rose from the dead so I could

be forgiven and have eternal life.
I confess that I have sinned and need Your mercy.
Thank You for loving me enough to die in my place.
I turn away from my old life and ask You to come into my heart and make me new.
I trust You as my Savior, and I choose to follow You as my Lord.
Thank You for saving me. I am Yours forever.
In Your name, Jesus, I pray. Amen.

If you prayed that sincerely from your heart, welcome to the family of God! Your journey of faith has just begun—and it's a journey that leads to life, purpose, and unshakable hope.

Journaling Prompts

1. What does the cross mean to me personally, and how has my view of it changed?

2. In what areas of my life do I still try to earn God's love instead of receiving His grace?

3. How can I live in response to Jesus' sacrifice in my everyday choices?

4. What does it mean to me that Jesus took my place on the cross?

5. Who in my life needs to hear about the love Jesus showed through His crucifixion, and how can I share it?

Epilogue

The End of the Questions… or the Beginning of the Journey?

You made it. Through the galaxies and gravity, the evidence and the eyewitnesses. Through black holes and Bible verses. From the edge of the cosmos to the foot of the cross.

But this isn't the end.

In fact, it might just be your beginning.

Somewhere along these pages, you may have found answers that surprised you—or raised even more questions. That's okay. Faith isn't about having it all figured out. It's about *trusting the One who does.*

You were created with a mind to explore, a heart to feel, and a soul that longs for something more. That longing? It's not a glitch. It's a clue. It's a whisper from the God who made you, knows you, and loves you more than you can imagine.

The same God who lit the stars also stepped into human skin. The one who wrote physics also wept at a grave. The one who hung the galaxies also hung on a cross—for you.

You don't have to be perfect to come to Him. You don't have to have all the answers, either. He's not asking you to be certain—He's inviting you to be honest.

So what now?

Now, you decide.
You can close this book and go back to life as usual.
Or you can take one bold, beautiful step closer to the God who has been pursuing you all along.

He's not just real.
He's *here*.
And He's calling your name.

Next Steps

What Now?

So you've read the evidence. You've wrestled with the big questions. Maybe you're feeling inspired, hopeful, challenged—or even overwhelmed. That's okay. You don't need to have everything figured out today. What matters is what you do with what you've discovered.

Here are some next steps to help you move forward—wherever you are in your journey:

1. Talk to God (Yes, for real.)

Prayer doesn't have to be fancy or memorized. Just talk to God like you would a trusted friend. Tell Him what you're thinking. Ask your questions. Even if you're not sure He's listening, try. Prayer is often the doorway to real relationship.

Example:

> "God, I'm not sure about everything, but I want to know You if You're real. Show me who You are. Help me understand what it means to follow You."

2. Say Yes to Jesus

If you believe Jesus is who He said He is—the Son of God who died for your sins and rose again—you can start a relationship with Him right now. You don't have to wait until you're "good enough." He came for the broken, the doubting, and the curious.

All it takes is a simple prayer of faith and surrender:

> "Jesus, I believe You are the Son of God. I believe You died and rose again for me. I'm sorry for living life my own way. I want to follow You. Be my Savior and my Lord. Help me trust You and walk with You."

If you prayed that and meant it, welcome to the family of God. Seriously. You're not alone anymore.

3. Read the Bible for Yourself

Start with the Gospel of John. It's a great place to get to know Jesus—who He is, what He said, and what He did. Don't worry if you don't understand everything at first. Ask God to speak to you as you read.

Consider journaling what you notice or how a verse speaks to your life. God's Word is living and personal—it will meet you where you are.

4. Find a Faith Community

You weren't made to walk this journey alone. Look for a local church, youth group, or trusted Christian mentor. Being around other believers will help you grow and give you a place to ask more questions, share struggles, and learn together.

If you're nervous, that's normal. But take the risk—God often meets us through people.

5. Keep Asking, Keep Growing

Following Jesus doesn't mean the questions stop. It means you now have a foundation to stand on while you keep learning. Faith is a journey, not a destination.

Stay curious. Stay humble. Keep seeking truth.

You're Not Alone

Whether you're on fire with faith, shaky with doubts, or somewhere in between, know this: God sees you. He loves you. And He's not done writing your story.

This book was just a beginning.
Now it's time for the next chapter—*yours*.

If you're ready to keep growing in your faith and understanding of the Bible, check out [Bible Chat's 3-Year Bible Chronological Daily]()

Devotional—a powerful, easy-to-follow resource that helps you read the Bible in the order events happened and reflect on what it means for your everyday life.

Also by the Author

3-Year Bible Chronological Daily Devotional (Year One)

Bible Chat's 3-Year Bible Chronological Daily Devotional (Year One) is your daily companion for a manageable and meaningful journey through God's Word.

Each devotional features short, reflective readings—perfect for your morning routine or quiet time. With a unique three-year Bible reading plan, you'll walk through the entire Old Testament in manageable segments, while the New Testament, Psalms, and Proverbs are revisited each year.

The devotional features:

- **Shorter Readings:** Designed to be easily incorporated into your daily routine, even on busy days. The shorter readings also allow for deeper reflection and meditation.
- **3-year Old Testament Plan:** The 3-Year Old Testament Plan offers shorter daily readings, covering Genesis to Judges in year one, Job to Solomon in year two, and the kings to Malachi in year three.
- **New Testament Focus:** Spend more time in the New Testament, immersing yourself in the teachings of Jesus and the early church.
- **Daily Proverbs:** One to two carefully selected proverbs each day provide bite-sized wisdom for daily living.
- **Chronological Arrangement:** Experience the unfolding narrative of Scripture by reading biblical stories and prophecies in their historical context. Discover fascinating connections,

Also By the Author

like reading the Psalm David wrote after hiding from Saul in a cave.

- **December's Christmas Devotional:** Journey through the anticipation of Christ's coming with readings that highlight God's plan of redemption throughout history.

At the end of each day's devotion, you will find *Think About It,* thoughtfully designed to deepen your engagement with the Scripture and the devotional message. These questions are an invitation to pause and reflect, helping you connect personally with God's Word and apply its timeless truths to your daily life. Whether used individually or in a group setting, these questions encourage you to examine your thoughts, actions, and faith journey, fostering spiritual growth and transformation.

Each day's devotion also includes a *Devotional Prayer*, inviting you to bring your reflections before God in a personal and heartfelt way. These prayers serve as a guide, helping you express your thoughts, desires, and concerns to God while aligning your heart with His will. They offer a powerful moment of connection with God, strengthening your faith and providing peace as you close each day in prayer.

Supplemented by the acclaimed *Bible Chat Podcast*, the *Bible Chat Daily Devotional* prioritizes a conversational and contemplative experience that fosters a deeper understanding of Scripture and its relevance to your life today.

FROM THE COSMOS TO THE CROSS

HOPE IN THE END:
A 31-DAY JOURNEY THROUGH THE END-TIMES

Are we living in the last days? What does Bible prophecy really mean — and why does it matter?

Hope in the End is a 31-day devotional that invites you to explore the End-Times through the lens of Scripture, not with fear or confusion, but with clarity, purpose, and unshakable hope. Rooted

Also By the Author

in the truth of God's Word, this devotional walks you through key end-time passages from Revelation, Daniel, the Gospels, and more — all pointing to one central figure: Jesus Christ, our soon-coming King.

Each daily reading includes:
- A focused Scripture passage
- A devotional reflection that reveals God's heart and plan
- A heartfelt prayer

Whether you're new to Bible prophecy or have studied it for years, **Hope in the End** will renew your vision of Christ's glory and prepare your heart to live with watchful faith, holy obedience, and confident expectation.

This isn't just a study of what's coming — it's a call to live differently *now*. **The end of the story is not darkness — it's hope. And that hope has a name: Jesus.**

Let this devotional strengthen your faith, steady your soul, and stir your heart to live every day in light of eternity.

From the Cosmos to the Cross

FREEDOM FIGHTERS:
HEROES OF FAITH WHO STOOD FOR TRUTH

A 42-Day Devotional Journey with Powerful Daily Prayers—for You and Your Nation!

What does real courage look like in a world that silences truth? How do you stand firm when everything around you tells you to compromise?

Also By the Author

<u>Freedom Fighters: Heroes of Faith Who Stood for Truth</u> is a powerful 42-day devotional that explores the lives of five extraordinary biblical figures—**Moses, Esther, Daniel, Paul, and Jesus**—each of whom stood boldly for truth in the face of fear, injustice, and opposition. Their stories weren't safe. They weren't easy. But they were full of purpose—and they're more relevant now than ever.

This devotional is more than just inspiration—it's a **call to action**. Each daily entry is designed to challenge your faith, strengthen your resolve, and stir your heart to live courageously in today's culture. You'll walk through:

- **Daily Scripture Readings** built around key Bible passages
- **Deep Reflections** rooted in timeless truth
- **Ponder and Reflection Questions** for spiritual growth
- **Powerful Personal Prayers** to help you respond in faith
- **Prayers for the Nation** to intercede for your country and community
- **Memorable Quotes** that inspire bold living

Whether you're leading a group, studying alone, or looking for a meaningful gift, *Freedom Fighters* will help you discover what it means to live for something greater than yourself.

www.ingramcontent.com/pod-product-compliance
Lightning Source LLC
Chambersburg PA
CBHW060756050426
42449CB00008B/1425